MOTOR AGE
FASHION

NANCY D. DeWITT

PHOTOS BY GREG MARTIN PHOTOGRAPHY

FOUNTAINHEAD ANTIQUE AUTO MUSEUM

Design: Elizabeth M. Watson, Watson Graphics
Publication management: Kent Sturgis Publishing Services, LLC
Digital prepress: William Campbell, Mars Premedia
Print production: Susan Dupèré

Library of Congress Control Number: 2016938722
ISBN: 978-0-692-68692-8
Photo Credit:
    Except as noted below, color photographs were taken by Greg Martin Photography, © 2016.
    Brian Bohannon: 107 (upper left)
    Michael Craft: 2, 6, 73 (Biddle), 127
    Nancy DeWitt: 13 (Hay), 28 (Columbia), 38 (Argo), 72 (Stutz), 87 (Stutz), 98 (Oakland), 103 (Stutz),
        110 (Hupmobile), 112 (Cadillac), 113 (Packard)
    Ronn Murray 45 (right), 120 (Packard)
    Willy Vinton: 61 (Peerless)

For more information about the publisher:
Fountainhead Antique Auto Museum
212 Wedgewood Drive
Fairbanks, Alaska 99701
(907) 450-2100
http://www.fountainheadmuseum.com
info@fountainheadmuseum.com

First Edition, 2016
10 9 8 7 6 5 4 3 2 1
Printed in China

■ FRONT COVER: Amy Hansen in a ca. 1926 evening dress with a 1925 Stutz Speedway Six Sportsbrohm
■ BACK COVER: Several "Good Time Girls" dressed up for an automobile ride in Fairbanks on June 21, 1910.

To our mothers born in the Roaring 20s
—Ruth, Connie, and Marjorie—for their
unfailing encouragement and support.
—Tim and Barb Cerny

■ RIGHT: **Jennie Johnson, Edith Ryan, and Mrs.**
Wallace Cathcart show off the latest fashions
in Albert Johnson's studio in Fairbanks, ca.
1907-1910. ALBERT JOHNSON PHOTOGRAPH COLLECTION
1989-166-298, ARCHIVES, UNIVERSITY OF ALASKA FAIRBANKS.

CONTENTS

■ LEFT: Page 14

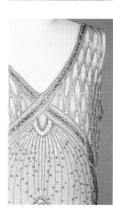

■ ABOVE: Page 83

■ RIGHT: Page 117

INTRODUCTION

A collection of antique cars and clothing may seem like an odd combination of artifacts to display together in a museum. Yet, automobile design and women's fashion were surprisingly intertwined during the early twentieth century. Both shared influences such as culture, wealth, war, and the Depression. Luxury cars and stylish clothing were each used as a means of self-expression and communicating social class. Some people even considered their automobile to be their final layer of clothing.

The automobile underwent tremendous changes during its early years, as did fashion. There were parallels in their overall designs, with the stiff, boxy look and eye-catching ornamentation of Brass era cars corresponding with the restricted silhouette and spectacular opulence of Late Victorian and early Edwardian fashions. As cars became faster and sportier, so did fashion, with racy, carefree dresses becoming prominent during the Roaring 20s. The 1930s were all about streamlining, with sculpted curves defining the elegant automobiles and gowns of the decade.

As the automobile grew in popularity, women's fashion adapted to this new form of transportation. Hemlines rose, corsets and dresses became less restrictive, and smaller hats came in vogue. Early automobiling was a dirty, dusty affair, so women added motoring bonnets, veils, and duster coats to their wardrobes. Beginning in the 1920s, some wealthy women collaborated with coachbuilders and

What started as a simple plan to display a dozen outfits blossomed into a genuine passion for historic costume by Barbara. Composed of more than 500 pieces dating from 1750 to the 1950s, the collection she assembled includes dresses, men's wear, undergarments, coats, sportswear, shoes, hats, hair pieces, purses, parasols, and jewelry.

The Cernys acquired the extensive clothing inventory from private collections and auction houses throughout North America. With over 100 outfits on display at a time, the museum's fashion collection is now among the largest on permanent display in the western United States.

The pieces selected for this book focus on women's wear from the late Victorian era through the 1930s, with an emphasis on Edwardian and 1920s fashion. Several automobiles from the museum are included, as are dresses and historic photographs from Alaska. Despite the rugged conditions of the Last Frontier, Alaska's pioneers were just as interested in fashion trends as their contemporaries in the States.

Together, these photographs illustrate how Western fashion changed dramatically during the first decades of the motor age, from excessively luxurious to streamlined sophistication.

couturiers to color coordinate their outfits with their custom-designed automobiles!

A captivating juxtaposition of vintage fashion and automobiles can be found at the Fountainhead Antique Auto Museum in Fairbanks, Alaska. Entrepreneur Tim Cerny and his wife, Barbara, opened the museum in 2009. Their original intention was to focus solely on pre-World-War II automobiles and Alaska motoring history. At the suggestion of several women in the local car club, Barbara and Tim decided to augment the exhibits with a small collection of vintage clothing.

■ **ABOVE: A fashionable group enjoys an outing in Bobby Sheldon's Pope Toledo car in Fairbanks in 1912.** PHOTO COURTESY OF THE FRANCES ERICKSON COLLECTION.

1. LATE VICTORIAN FASHIONS

The Victorian era (~1837-1901), named for Queen Victoria of England, was a time of some of the most confining fashions ever worn by Western women. The favorable silhouettes emphasized a woman's bust, waist, and hips, with the desired shapes initially achieved by heavily boned corsets, protruding bustles, and large hoop skirts.

By the 1890s, crinolines and bustles had fallen out of fashion. Extremely tight corseting helped a woman achieve the preferred hourglass figure, with her tiny waist offset by decorated bodices and simple, flared skirts.

Late Victorian day dresses had high-necked, tight-fitting bodices that could be very elaborate, with frills, tucks, lace, embroidery, and epaulettes for trim. Sleeves grew very large during this time, reaching enormous proportions by 1895. Called leg o' mutton or gigot sleeves, some were so immense that they required 2½ yards of material each!

Evening gowns had lower necklines and short sleeves of lace or extravagant puffs. Hats were small but usually quite ornate. By day, women wore boots or button shoes, some with remarkably high heels. Evening shoes had lower, curved French heels.

The late Victorian and Edwardian eras (1890-1914) encompassed a period of prosperity, extravagance, and style known as the La Belle Époque, meaning the Beautiful Era. It was a time of luxurious fashion and the introduction of a revolutionary form of transportation—the automobile.

■ **LEFT: 1895 two-piece afternoon dress made of brown satin brocade with blue spiral roundels, A BLUE satin high collar and lapels, and leg o' mutton sleeves.**
■ **ABOVE TOP: ca. 1890 black straw bonnet with pink silk floral decoration. Displayed on a Victorian wax bust.**
■ **ABOVE: ca. 1900-1910 leather two-tone, lace-up boots with brown and gold print fabric uppers.**

■ ABOVE: Francis Tuttle with tourists and some of his crew on the revenue cutter *U.S.S. Bear* en route to Alaska, ca. 1897-1900. The women are wearing a late Victorian style cape (left) and traveling coats with leg o' mutton sleeves (center and right). EDWARD MULLIGAN PHOTOGRAPH ALBUM 1961-1018-57, ARCHIVES, UNIVERSITY OF ALASKA FAIRBANKS.

1894-1895 Afternoon Gown
A million years in the making

ca. 1893 Girl's Party Dress
Petite belle of the ball

Victorian mourning etiquette required that an upper class widow wear black for two years. For the first year, only dull fabrics such as crepe or bombazine (a type of twilled fabric) were acceptable. After one year, a widow could add ornamentation to her mourning dress; by 21 months she could wear dresses made from lustrous black fabrics such as taffeta and velvet.

Voluminous sleeves, as seen on this late-stage mourning gown, were often accompanied by elaborate bodice decorations or jewelry. Beautiful jet beads adorn the bodice of this black velvet dress. Jet is a type of gemstone formed from wood that decayed under extreme pressure during the Jurassic period. This intensely dark, "jet black" gem was very popular during Queen Victoria's reign, especially for mourning jewelry.

■ RIGHT: Girls' dresses incorporated the fashions of the Victorian period, including leg o' mutton sleeves and flared skirts. This one was constructed from iridescent blue silk and finished with an eye-catching sash of red velvet.

1898 Hay Motor Vehicle

■ **ABOVE:** Chatelaines were decorative clasps worn on a woman's waistband. Several chains were attached to the clasp, to which useful items such as keys, scissors, and small purses could be attached. This ca. 1890s chatelaine purse has a gold-plated carry chain and frame embossed with open filigree. The bag is decorated with jet beads and an interlocking beaded fringe
■ **BELOW:** ca. 1890s velvet and fur carriage boots, worn as overshoes over a lady's delicate, indoor-only slippers.

1893-1895 Evening Gown
Custom made for the miners' sweetheart

The label on this vivid, two-piece silk dress fashioned with latticed bands of crimson velvet reads "Chas. A. Stevens & Brothers," which was a Chicago department store. It was reportedly owned by Colorado resident Elizabeth McCourt Tabor, best known as Baby Doe and once called "the best dressed woman in the West."

Baby Doe was the second wife of wealthy silver magnate Horace Tabor, whom she married following their scandalous affair. The couple lived a lavish lifestyle, and Baby Doe gained a reputation as one of the most beautiful, flamboyant, and alluring women in the West.

At one point the Tabors were among the five wealthiest families in the country, but they lost their fortune following the repeal of the Sherman Silver Act and subsequent Panic of 1893. Both died destitute, Horace in 1899 and Baby Doe in 1935.

This was perhaps one of the last fine dresses purchased by Baby Doe before she lost her wealth. It is a busy gown with so many textures and accents, but quite appropriate for an ostentatious millionaire nicknamed the "miners' sweetheart."

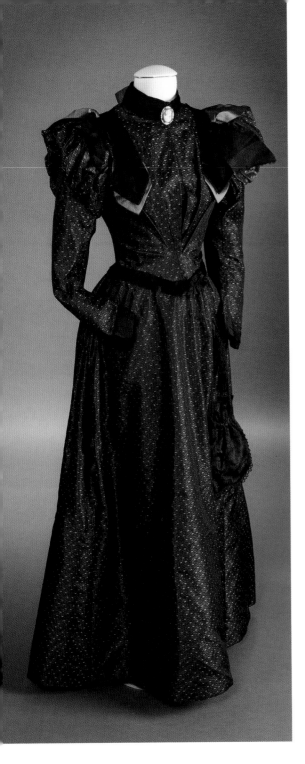

ca. 1898 Day Dress
Wide shoulders were all the rage

■ ABOVE: CA. 1890-1900 black silk shoes with Louis heels from the Aristo Marshall Fields Co. The oversized tongues are decorated with jet beads.

This dress has a tightly boned bodice, which along with its leg o' mutton sleeves and bell-shaped skirt, helped create the hourglass silhouette so prized in the 1890s. The heavy chestnut silk brocade with black serpentines and white dots is reminiscent of the Victorian "style tapissier" (literally, upholsterer's fashion), in which dress fabrics—stiff satins, tapestries, taffeta, and jacquards—mimicked household upholstery and draperies. The black and copper silk satin ribbon accents gives the dress just the right touch of jaunty femininity.

■ ABOVE: ca. 1890 silk mourning parasol with a folding wooden handle.

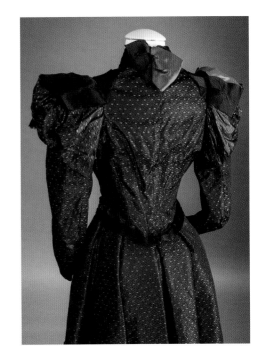

1898-1899 Day Dress
Sumptuous Victorian frills

Victorian fashion dictated that women of means wear specific styles of dress for day, evening, at-home wear, and different outings. A day dress typically had a high neck and long sleeves. This lovely, two-piece dress is made from an interesting material with a woven, quilt-like surface. The claret-colored bodice and skirt are accented by lace, velvet trim, silk bow appliqués, and sheer silk ruching.

An attached, black silk mantelet with fabulous ruching and long lappets drapes over the shoulders. A Victorian bonnet with silk flowers and ribbon completes the ensemble.

2. TURN-OF-THE-CENTURY CORSETS

Corsets and girdles have been used for centuries to mold women's (and sometimes men's) figures into the fashionable shape of the times. The two corsets shown on these pages created dramatically different silhouettes.

During the late Victorian period, the fashionable shape included a well-developed bust, tapered waist, and large hips representing a mature woman. A steel spoon busk in the front of the corset carved the stomach inward, cupped the lower abdomen, and pushed the bulk of the flesh up and down to create the desired hourglass silhouette. The stiff corset along with a gown's lavish embellishments, heavy fabrics, and elaborate underpinnings made it difficult for a woman to do much more than walk and sit.

In 1901, a fresh look arrived that greatly contrasted to the upright silhouette of the previous decades. The new, straight busk corset pushed the bosom forward and forced

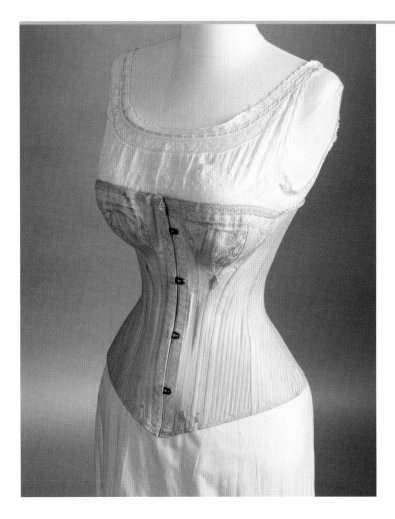

the hips back, creating an "S-bend" silhouette. The corset sat below the bust, producing a low, mono-bosom look emphasized by drooping bodices said to resemble pigeons' breasts.

This new corset was supposed to be more healthful than the spoon busk, which many believed displaced a woman's internal organs. In actuality, this corset allowed for even tighter cinching and caused back, breathing, and knee hyperextension problems. What was deemed the "health corset" actually turned out to be the most harmful accessory Western women had used to force their figures into a desired silhouette.

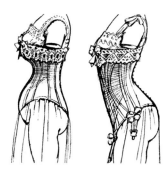

■ Spoon busk versus straight busk corset.

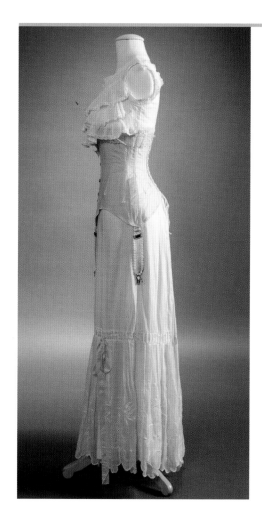

3. EARLY EDWARDIAN FASHIONS

The early Edwardian era introduced a period of very luxurious and cumbersome fashion. From approximately 1901 to 1908, the ideal look was that of a curvy, mature woman. Health corsets forced the body into an S-shape with a low, mono-bosom pushed forward and the derrière thrust backward. Women created a pigeon breast look by wearing outer bodices that were cut longer in the front so they drooped over the waistband. These were often further enhanced with pouches of lace or gathered fabric.

Bodices elongated the neck by having extremely high collars supported by silk-covered wires. Sleeves were blousy, ending in gathers at the wrists. Outer bodices were usually attached to heavily boned under-bodices that provided extra contour to achieve the S-shape.

Early Edwardian skirts swept over a full behind, down or in toward the knees, and then flared gracefully at the hemline. Skirts typically brushed the floor or ended in a train.

The forward tilt of a woman's torso created by the straight busk corset could be so severe that many women used beautiful canes or parasols for balance. They wore large, lavishly decorated hats that required big pompadour hairstyles and hatpins as long as 18 inches to support them.

By day, women typically wore button or lace-up boots. Court shoes with curved Louis heels and embellished with embroidery, beading, or metallic thread, were worn with eveningwear.

■ Left: Blue silk faille skirt with a fringed crochet apron, paired with an ivory silk satin blouse showing a drooping pigeon breast.
■ Top: Felted beaver hat trimmed with pheasant, turkey, and ostrich feathers, ca. 1900-1910.
■ Bottom: Button-strap shoes were worn throughout the Edwardian era. These ca. 1910 Sorosis evening shoes in dove gray suede have Louis heels and decorative cutwork on the vamps (upper surfaces). The straps and vamps feature cut steel beadwork.

■ Above: The second annual Grand Ball of the Tanana Masonic Club of Fairbanks, February 22, 1906. Rust Family Papers 1963-0054-44, Archives, University of Alaska Fairbanks.

ca. 1902-1904 Afternoon Dress
Dripping with Edwardian extravagance

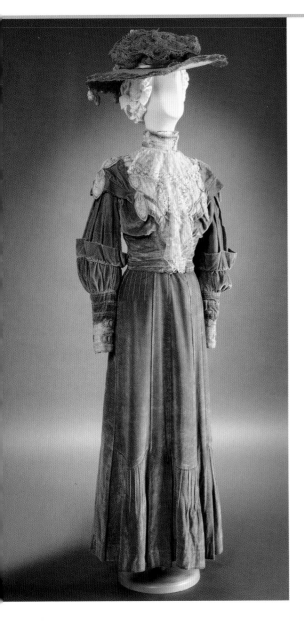

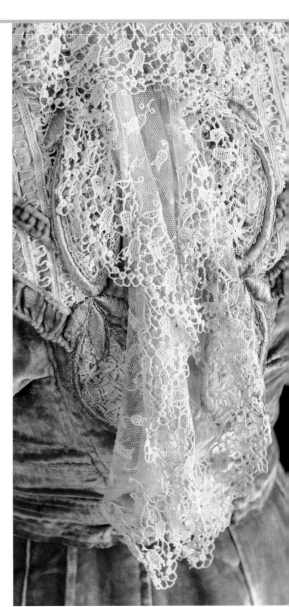

The elaborate embellishments on this sage green velvet gown illustrate the opulence typical of La Belle Époch. Appliqué and a cascade of lace decorate the highly tailored bodice, accompanied by bishop-style sleeves with lace cuffs. Darts, pleats, and the V-shaped lace insert in the back accentuate the narrow waist.

The ca. 1900-1908 hat shown with this ensemble is an intricately woven, open work straw hat trimmed with sea green crimped silk ribbon. Silk fabric cocoons drape gracefully from the back.

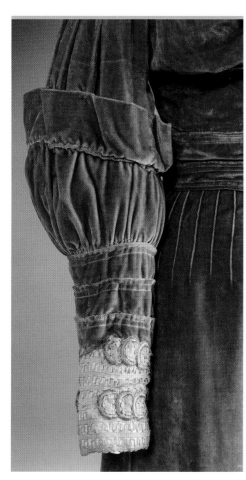

■ Right Top: Victorian wicker purse shaped like an umbrella with a drawstring opening around the bamboo handle. Decorated with eyelet lace and silk flowers.

■ Right: ca. 1910 lace-up boots with tall Louis heels and decorative punch work in the sage green leather. This style of footwear appeared in the late 1800s and carried over into the Edwardian era.

1901-1903 Day Dress
A ray of sunshine on the promenade

Imagine seeing a woman strolling along the promenade in this radiant dress! The bodice is made from figured yellow silk set off by contrasting black lace appliqué and velvet trim, an attached white chiffon shoulder scarf, and a cream lace yoke. The skirt of silk faille (a heavyweight and subtly ribbed silk) has ruffled tiers and a slight train. A straw hat adorned with silk ribbon, cloth flowers, and a dyed ostrich plume completes the ensemble.

ca. 1901-1902 Day Dress
Girlish charm in pink ribbon and lace

The small size of this lingerie dress and its alternating rows of pink ribbon and lace fabric indicate it was made for a teenaged girl. The pink ribbons, delicate lace and appliqué bodice, lace cuffs, and lace waist radiate charm and femininity. It would be hard to not take note of a young lady wearing this delightful frock!

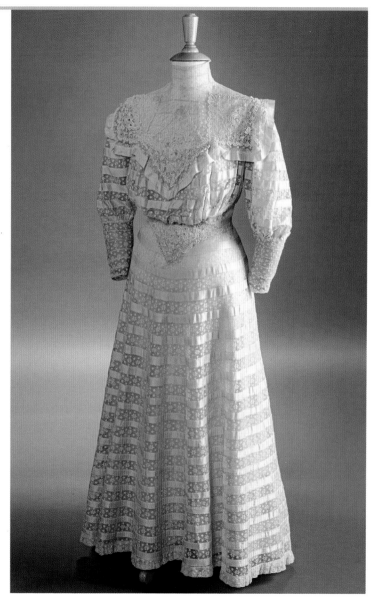

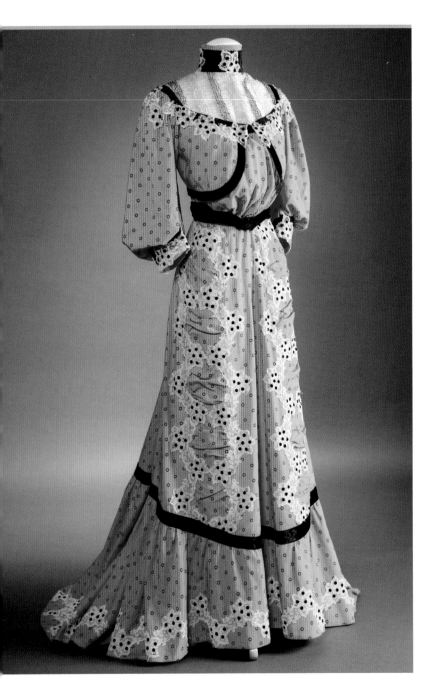

1904 Afternoon Gown
Gibson Girl beauty in pink

This trained dress conjures visions of the classic Gibson Girl—the romantic icon of feminine beauty created by illustrator Charles Dana Gibson. She was statuesque and slender, with her torso shaped into a fashionable S-curve to highlight her ample bosom and narrow waist.

This vibrant, geranium pink gown is made from a gauzy, open-weave wool called nun's veiling. It is embellished with a shirred ecru silk neckline, lace appliqués, and black velvet trim and dots. The trumpet-shaped skirt culminates in a long train, which was popular even on daytime wear.

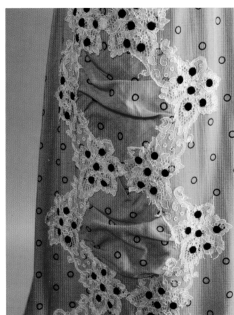

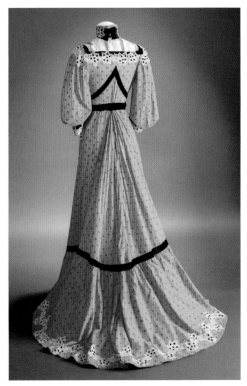

ca. 1904 Evening Gown
Couture in cream silk and black lace

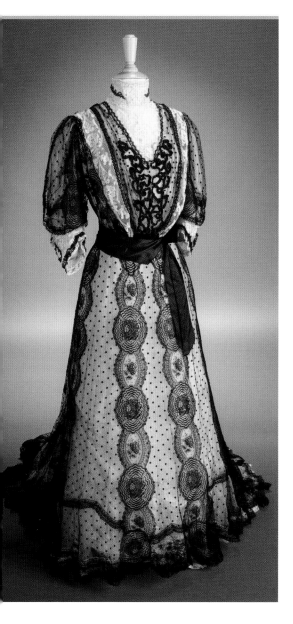

The museum's couture collection includes this lovely Callot Soeurs dress from France. The Callot sisters were renowned for their extraordinary technique that combined lush fabrics like silk, satin, brocade, and gold lamé with antique lace, lavish beading, and intricate embroidery.

This trained evening gown has an underskirt made from cream taffeta-like silk, which is overlain with a delicate layer of silk gauze and lace-adorned tulle. The handmade laces forming the chain-like pattern and the skirt's border are made up of exquisite floral designs. Other delicate laces adorn the bodice and sleeves.

1905-1907 Day Dress

Stylish mourning wear

T he drooping pigeon breast popular during the early
Edwardian era is evident on this mourning dress made
of black satin, lace, and taffeta. Several tiers of lightweight
silk tulle enhance the flounced skirt, which has a small train.
Lace insets on the bodice and at the ends of the elbow-
length sleeves add striking contrast on this lovely frock.

■ Top Right: 1903 Columbia electric surrey

1906 Tea Gown
Stylish comfort for the elegant hostess

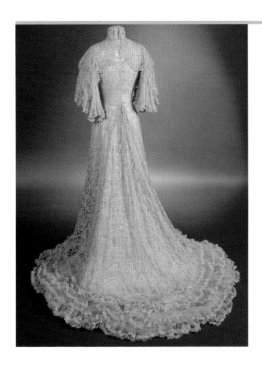

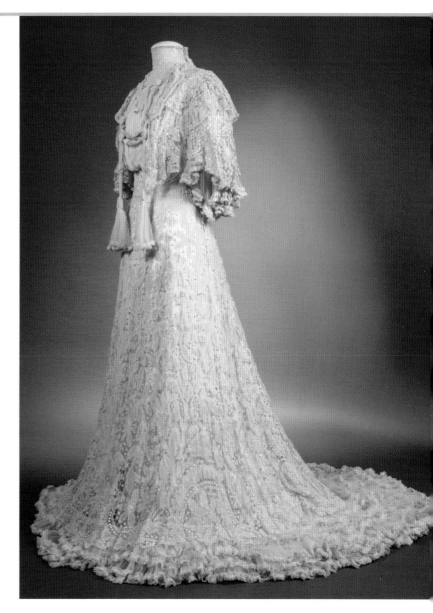

Tea gowns, popular among prominent women, could be worn without a corset and were therefore a more comfortable form of dress for receiving guests at home. Tea gowns had long, flowing sleeves and a train, and the more luxurious ones were decorated with abundant laces and frills.

This ultra-feminine dress may have been worn as a tea gown, but its fitted bodice indicates it required a corset. It is covered with Battenberg lace, which combined machine-woven tapes with hand stitching. Valenciennes lace inserts, a pleated neckline, elegant tassels,

and several ruffled flounces on the voluminous skirt make this one of the most stunning gowns in the Fountainhead Collection.

■ ABOVE: ca. 1900 ivory satin wedding shoes decorated with bows and beaded embroidery.

■ **Above: Two women wearing different styles of walking suits stroll on the boardwalk in Valdez, ca. 1912.** P.S. Hunt, photographer. Mary Whalen Photograph Collection 1975-84-62, Archives, University of Alaska Fairbanks.

4. OUTDOOR WEAR AND WALKING SUITS

By the end of the nineteenth century, middle and upper class women were actively participating in exercise and leisure activities. This called for new additions to their wardrobes in the form of outerwear, underwear, and sportswear.

A striking contrast to the feminine frills of the Edwardian era was the masculine outfit called the tailor-made, or walking suit. Consisting of a straight skirt and a matching jacket, these outfits were originally designed for travel, although the skirt could be shortened to ankle-length for outdoor activities and motoring. Wool, tweed, and linen were the fabrics of choice for tailor-mades.

Increasingly independent women found the tailor-made a useful, all-purpose outfit, especially among those entering the workforce. Many others, however, considered the tailor-made unladylike and did not like the statement of blossoming female independence it signified.

■ LEFT: 1905-1908 wool walking suit. The tailored jacket has a cutaway front, velvet placket and collar, and a lining of beautifully patterned silk. On loan from the Pioneers of Alaska, Women's Igloo #8.

■ RIGHT: Labeled "Franklin Simon & Co. Fifth Avenue New York," this 1910 linen walking suit consists of a loose fitting, box-style jacket and long skirt decorated with mother-of-pearl buttons.

ca. 1900s Winter Wear
Skirting the cold and dirt

This stylish ensemble, on loan from the Pioneers of Alaska, Women's Igloo #8, would have been appropriate for a cold winter day. The heavy brown jacket of silk brocade dates to 1904. Trimmed with black silk frog closures, a black silk collar, and upturned cuffs, the jacket was not only practical but also fashionable.

For extra warmth, women wore soft wool petticoats under their outer petticoats and dresses. This ca. 1900 red wool flannel petticoat with contrasting black embroidery is displayed underneath a brown wool skirt from 1901.

A pair of small tongs with padded circular discs, known as a dress lifter, was used to keep skirts clear of dirt or when climbing stairs, riding, or bicycling. It hung from a chain or cord attached to a waistband or chatelaine, often alongside other useful items such as scissors, pencils, keys, and a small purse. The wearer could slide the top piece of the dress lifter to open or lock closed the pincers, which attached to the hem of the skirt. A pull on the cord or chain lifted the skirt free of the ground and the ever-present mud and dirt.

1905 Walking Suit
Made for work, travel, or a stroll

This wool ensemble shows the waist-length jacket style that was fashionable for early Edwardian walking suits. The gored skirt was made of several triangular panels that flattered the waist and hips while allowing for ease of movement.

The bolero-style bodice is trimmed with black and ivory satin, military braid, decorative tabs, and fabric-covered buttons. The back of the bodice is as interesting as the front, embellished with pleats, a self-fabric panel, and decorations of black fabric buttons.

Walking suits were decorated front and back, as it was important for a woman to look attractive from all angles.

ca. 1910 Skating Ensemble

"Skating is an art to which all ladies should attain." - The Eclectic Magazine

This full-length, cashmere wool coat was designed to be worn while ice-skating. It is lined in cream satin and has a fox fur collar.

The coat is displayed with a two-piece wool day dress with a number of fascinating construction details. The high-necked bodice insert and cuffs are made from ivory silk overlaid with pastel-colored lace. The bodice is further accented with satin-covered buttons, silk piping, decorative tabs, and diagonal pleats. Seven lines of boning circumscribe the interior of the bodice, which fastens with a series of hooks and eyes down the back.

■ RIGHT: Beaver fur has long been prized for its warmth, luxurious texture, and durability. Many men's top hats were made from felted beaver fur. This ca. 1900–1905 lady's winter hat is made from plush beaver felt and is adorned with ostrich plumes dyed brown and tan.

■ Above: Four women laugh while ice-skating on the frozen Chena River in Fairbanks on March 27, 1910. Photo courtesy of Candy Waugaman.

ca. 1909 Walking Suit
Tailor made for an Alaska lady

This wool gabardine walking suit came from Gordon's Department Store in Fairbanks. A native of Scotland, F.S. Gordon landed in Valdez in February 1905 with wooden crates full of merchandise. He bought several horses to carry the crates and then led them on foot over 375 miles (603 km) to Fairbanks, where he opened a store on Cushman Street. His first sale was a petticoat, for which he received gold dust in payment.

Gordon was known for giving away grand prizes, including gold dust and a piano, as incentives to purchase goods from his store. He served as the mayor of Fairbanks from 1911 to 1912.

This well-preserved suit is on loan from the Pioneers of Alaska, Women's Igloo #8.

1909-1910 Walking Suit
Treasured by an Alaska Pioneer

This lovely green tailor-made belonged to Alaska pioneer Louise Walsh (née Forsythe). Louise was born in 1886 in Massachusetts and in 1899 became the first Caucasian girl to arrive in Nome. In 1909 she married an Irish miner named Mike Walsh. This suit may have been part of her wedding trousseau.

The couple lived in Nome, where Mike was the city clerk from 1931-1944. A delegate to Alaska's Constitutional Convention, Mike also served in Alaska's Territorial House of Representatives and as a member of the Board of Regents for the University of Alaska. Both Mike and Louise were very active in the Pioneers of Alaska, of which Mike was Grand President in 1954.

Louise and Mike raised ten children. Theirs was the largest family of children to receive high school diplomas in Alaska before statehood. Mike died in 1963, and Louise passed away in 1971.

This suit is trimmed with black bengaline and shown with an ivory crepe blouse. The suit was generously donated by Louise and Mike's grandson, Kevin Walsh, and his wife, Linda, to the Fountainhead Antique Auto Museum.

■ **ABOVE: Multi-bar evening shoes with decorated straps first appeared in the 1880s, and then periodically throughout the Edwardian era. They reached the height of their popularity when hemlines rose during the Teens.**

ca. 1914 Walking Suit
Military-inspired fashion

After the Great War began in 1914, it was not uncommon to see military influences in fashion. This silk velvet suit, labeled "B. Altman & Co. Paris New York," carries an intricate, military-style pattern of cord on the long, A-line skirt and collarless jacket.

The jacket's front edges, hem, and sleeves are decorated in gold cord swirls and diamond shapes. Cord-covered frog closures sit below the paisley vest insert that is adorned with self-fabric buttons. The sides of the skirt carry wing-like cord decorations, and a deep band of pleats is found on the back hem.

■ BELOW: 1913 Argo electric fore-drive limousine

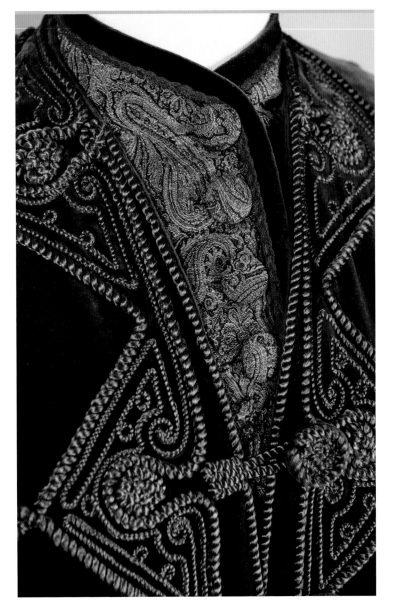

■ ABOVE: Brown velvet turban-style hat, ca. 1911, decorated with green-dyed ostrich feathers and a brown satin bow.

■ ABOVE: **Friends on the boardwalk in Nome, July 4, 1910.** SIEFFERT FAMILY PHOTOGRAPHS 1985-122-37, ARCHIVES, UNIVERSITY OF ALASKA FAIRBANKS.

5. BEAUTY AND THE BIRD

Feathers, Fashion, and Our Fowl Obsession

Birds have captivated humans for centuries. We have caged them, decorated our homes with their likeness, and written countless songs and poems extolling their beauty. We have also used these feathered jewels for personal adornment, both in imitation and natural form.

Feathers have especially fascinated us and been used to symbolize wealth, status, and fashion among many cultures. By the late Victorian era it had become fashionable to wear extravagant arrangements on large hats, composed not just of feathers but sometimes heads, wings, and even entire birds.

The plume trade reached its peak during the late 1890s, when over five million birds were being killed annually to supply the millinery (hat-making) industry. Many bird populations were driven to or towards extinction as a result. At greatest risk were America's egrets,

Britain's gulls and terns, Africa's wild ostrich herds, and New Guinea's birds-of-paradise.

Horror over such wholesale destruction of bird populations awakened a conservation ethic that still resonates today. In 1896, Boston socialite Harriet Hemenway and her cousin Minna Hall spoke at a series of afternoon teas about the cruelty of the plume trade. Their efforts persuaded 900 influential society women to boycott the wearing of feathered hats.

Hemenway and Hall also created the first Audubon Society, which promoted the wearing of "Audubonnets." These large hats were festooned with ribbons and other decorations in place of feathers, or adorned with "acceptable" feathers from ducks, geese, pheasants, and farmed ostriches.

■ Above left: ca. 1907-1910 black straw hat decorated with black netting, ostrich plumes, and the head and nape from a sooty tern. Label reads "Fernande, Paris, 52 Boul'd Maussmann."

■ Left: ca. 1907 black straw hat with velvet lining, trimmed in black ostrich feathers and pink silk and sateen roses.

By the turn of the century, 16 Audubon societies had formed across the country to demand an end to the plume trade. Audubon members successfully lobbied Congress to pass the 1900 Lacey Act, which prohibited interstate commerce of wild fowl and game. Additional bird protection laws, the rising popularity of the automobile, a shift in society's attitudes, and the introduction of the bobbed hairstyle finally led to the end of this "murderous millinery."

■ Right: Black felted beaver fur hat trimmed in black silk ribbon set with a rhinestone buckle. Iridescent green and black rooster feathers and a spray of egret feathers dyed black accent the brim.

■ Right: ca. 1912–1914 brown felted wool pot hat trimmed in ochre and ruby velvet and decorated with the heads and tail feathers from two pheasants.

■ Right: ca. 1900 tricorn hat made of silk satin and decorated with dyed aigrettes.

■ LEFT: ca. 1910–1912 gold lace and net hat trimmed with a lesser bird-of-paradise. The label reads "Lane-Walsh Millinery."
■ RIGHT: ca. 1910 lilac straw hat with purple-dyed bird wings, pink-dyed rooster feathers, a lilac chiffon scarf, and large silver buckle.

■ LEFT: Forest green silk turban with braided straw accents and an orange and green iridescent plume made from Asian pheasant feathers.
■ RIGHT: Black straw hat with dyed ostrich and fowl feathers and a beaded ornament, ca. 1910. DONATED BY THE LOFTUS ESTATE TO THE PIONEER MUSEUM.

Text within the photograph:
VALDEZ & FAIRBANKS
AUTO TRANS. CO.

AUTO PARTY AT VALDE GLACIER,
JULY 11-09.

P.S. HUNT
C 2289.

■ ABOVE: A smartly dressed group chartered this White steam car for a tour to Valdez Glacier on July 4, 1909. WICKERSHAM STATE HISTORIC SITE PHOTOGRAPHS PCA-277-014-030, ALASKA STATE LIBRARY.

6. LATE EDWARDIAN FASHIONS

By 1908, fashion had taken a healthier but equally uncomfortable direction. The new ideal silhouette became long and slim. Corsets did away with severe lacing and began to lengthen and straighten, starting just above the waist and reaching well down the thighs. Though they no longer hampered breathing, corsets were so long and tight over the hips that sitting was difficult.

Women typically wore these long corsets under single-piece dresses with high, empire waists and flowing skirts. These gowns were reminiscent of the Directoire and Empire styles of the late 1700s and early 1800s.

Dresses were made of light materials, often layered and sewn in asymmetrical patterns. Ankle-length day dresses, especially tunic-style ones, were common. Walking suits, blouses with skirts, and lingerie dresses covered with lace trim rose in popularity for daywear.

By day, women wore huge Merry Widow hats to offset their narrow, column-like silhouettes. Many hats, like the one shown at right, carried an abundance of decorations, such as flowers, lace, fruit, and feathers. Those that lacked these ornate trimmings compensated by being extremely wide, like the oversize straw boater hat above. Smaller hats were reserved for motoring and horseback riding.

Evening dresses were made of light or sheer fabrics adorned with lace or other trimmings over a silk underlayer. Most were floor-length, and many had trains. Hats were not worn with evening gowns. Instead, it was fashionable to adorn one's pompadour hairstyle with elaborate combs, jewels, aigrettes, feathers, or a tiara.

ca. 1908 Ball Gown

Heavy on the details

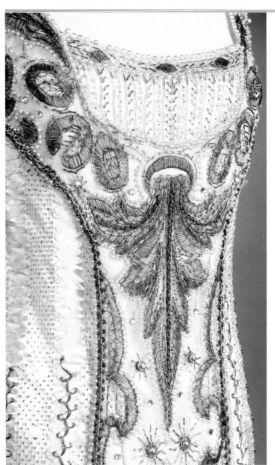

Every detail of this luscious, one-piece gown is a feast for the eyes. The beaded net and tulle overdress is beautifully embellished with silver and gold beading, embroidery, rhinestones, pearls, bronze thread, and white silk ribbon. No doubt the wearer of this lovely dress stood out from the crowd!

The abundance of decorations made this gown very heavy—over 8 lbs. (3.6 kg), in fact. The wearer could hold up the fishtail train with the hidden wrist loop, but even that must have been tiring after a few minutes.

■ ABOVE: Hand-painted silk fans with mother-of-pearl handles, ca. 1900.

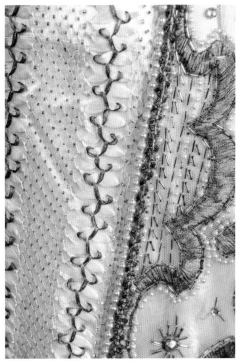

1909-1911 Evening Gown
Reminiscent of the Renaissance

The aesthetic dress movement that arose in the 1860s likely inspired this trained gown. The aesthetic style rejected tight corseting and favored beautiful materials and the loose, flowing lines reminiscent of medieval and Renaissance dresses. Fabric colors tended to be muted and natural toned, giving garments the appearance of being old and faded.

The bodice on this delicate crepe de chine gown is trimmed with gold lace and a lamé front apron edged with five gold tassels. Fabric-wrapped cord swirls and silk brocade panels in the front and back further enhance the beauty of this romantic dress.

■ LEFT: 1915 silver lamé evening shoes. Simple pumps with curved Louis heels such as these were in fashion throughout the Belle Époch.

1913 Dinner Gown
Sophistication in Chantilly lace

A wealth of brightly colored silk and contrasting lace characterize this gorgeous, one-piece gown. Its pleated, black net sleeves and yards of black Chantilly lace overlay the chartreuse silk bengaline (a strong ribbed fabric made from a mixture of silk and either cotton or wool). The sequined, cream lace neck insert edged in paste jewels and black velvet, green silk waistband, and vivid chartreuse train provide a striking contrast to the dark lace. For a final touch, long lace streamers sweep from the filigree and paste buckle in back.

ca. 1910 Day Dress
Cheerful florals of silk floss

Although not as elaborate as evening gowns, Edwardian day dresses were rarely plain. The natural-colored silk fabric of this dress is trimmed in large flowers embroidered from beige silk floss. The seams, lace yoke, and lace under-sleeves are trimmed with eye-catching piping made from copper-colored fabric.

■ TOP RIGHT: ca. 1910 beaver fur-trimmed hat with pink silk roses, white silk ribbon, and ostrich feathers dyed black.

■ RIGHT: 1912 Premier 6-60 roadster

ca. 1912 Day Dress
Stylish silk, soutache, and lace

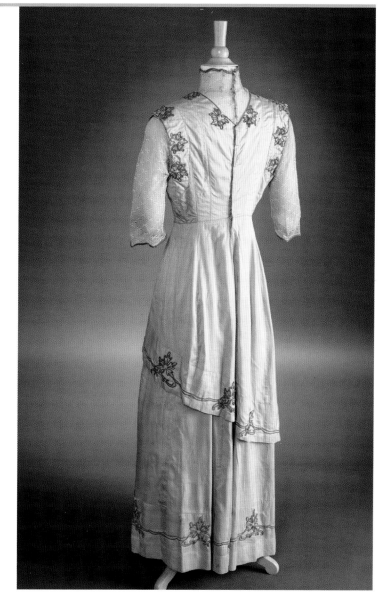

A delightful profusion of hand-embroidered soutache flower motifs highlight this one-piece dress made from natural silk. The asymmetrical, partial overskirt, also trimmed in soutache, extends around the back from the front panel. The yoke and ¾-length sleeves are composed of machine-made lace, edged with tan cord.

1909-1912 Evening Gown
Ivory and gold for a night at the opera

At first glance, this Titanic era opera gown seems extraordinarily plain for evening-wear. It boasts no shimmering beads or sequins, no jewel-toned satins or elaborate lace. Its most prominent decorative detail is an abundance of embroidery in golden silk floss.

And yet, the gown's artful design blossoms with femininity and poise. Such apparent simplicity would focus attention on the natural beauty of the woman who wore it, rather than on her costume.

The gown's lithe silhouette features an empire waist, minimal boning, and a softly gathered cummerbund culminating in a pearl-trimmed silk corsage at the back. The lines of the dress follow the natural, graceful curves of the body. A cutaway tunic covers the slender skirt, falling gently from knee length in front to a train in the back.

A charming lady draped in this uncomplicated gown might well have outshone all the other glittering women at the opera.

ca. 1913 Dinner Gown
The delight is in the details

From the embroidered silk rose accents on the skirt to the pompom-fringed sleeves, this gown radiates exquisite craftsmanship and Titanic era style. Its higher neck and longer sleeves distinguish it from the low-cut ball gowns of the era. The black lace net outer layer is embellished with black velvet, charcoal and ivory beads, and embroidery of copper, green, and gold lamé. Two straps of ivory cutwork lace peek through the netting on the bodice, while silk ribbon bands overlay the netting on each sleeve. Silk roses highlight the top of the side split in the overskirt, where bands of silk ribbon adorned with black glass buttons and beads are revealed underneath.

■ **Above:** A group of ladies enjoy a garden party in Fairbanks, ca. 1912. Most are wearing lingerie dresses, which must have been comfortable during warm summer days in Alaska's Interior. PHOTO COURTESY OF CANDY WAUGAMAN.

7. EDWARDIAN LINGERIE DRESSES

From about 1897 through 1915, a common dress style worn by women of all ages was the white, lace-trimmed gown known as a lingerie dress. As their name implied, these gauzy confections—decorated with white embroidery, eyelets, ribbons, pintucks, and lace inserts—resembled undergarments. Although a white dress once symbolized wealth, a farmer's wife was as likely to wear a lingerie dress as was a high society lady.

Unlike the hard-to-wash silk, velvet, satin, and wool dresses of the time, lingerie dresses were usually fashioned from batiste (a thin, opaque cotton), soft organdy, voile, or lawn (similar to batiste). They were also easy to make, thanks to readily available patterns, machine-constructed laces, and sewing machines. Women could sew a dress, stitch the lace in place, and then simply cut away the fabric beneath it.

Lingerie dresses were among the first mass-produced dresses and could be purchased through mail-order catalogs. At the turn of the century, more than half of the dresses offered in the Sears, Roebuck & Co. catalog were made of white, lace-trimmed cloth ranging in price from $4.75 to $11.

Lingerie dresses were popular among Alaska's pioneer women, even in the mining camps. Although they soiled easily, the lightweight fabrics were easy to wash at home.

■ LEFT: 1905 white batiste lingerie dress with floral embroidery, lace open cutwork, and a neckline, lower sleeves, and horizontal skirt panel of lace.

■ ABOVE TOP: Lace and embroidery detail on 1905 lingerie dress shown at left.
■ ABOVE: Waiting for the boat after a picnic outing to Knik. FALCON JOSLIN PAPERS 1979-41-337, ARCHIVES, UNIVERSITY OF ALASKA FAIRBANKS.

1910-1912 Lingerie Dresses
"Underwear as outwear"

■ LEFT and above: ca. 1910 lingerie dress with intricate open lace and pintucks on the sleeves and bodice sides. The skirt is decorated with multiple pintucks, a horizontal lace insert, and lace gathered delicately at the waist. Fairbanks resident Sharon Cook, whose grandmother wore this for her wedding in the Upper Midwest, donated this dress.

■ RIGHT: ca. 1910 hat of pink straw trimmed with large cabbage roses, leaves, and black velvet ribbons.

■ RIGHT: ca. 1912 lingerie dress showing the higher, empire waist and straighter, sleeker look of the late Edwardian period. The skirt falls from the natural waistline seam with alternating vertical rows of insertion lace and batiste that elongated the figure.

ca. 1915 Lingerie Dress
Ruffles and organdy for graduation

■ **Above: Three young ladies look lovely in their high-school graduation dresses and sashes in Fairbanks. They appear to be wearing the "cootie garage" or "earphone" hairstyle that was popular in the late Teens and early 1920s. The style involved coiling long hair into two buns over each ear.** Gaustad-Bartlett Family Papers 1972-0156-147, Archives, University of Alaska Fairbanks.

Lingerie dresses were popular among teenagers and were often worn during high-school graduation ceremonies. This young lady's dress is made from sheer white cotton organdy trimmed in tiers of self-fabric ruffles that match the frilly sleeves and neckline.

The dress is very similar to the one worn by the young lady in the photo at left. The girls' dresses show the new hemline of the Teens, which by 1915 had risen dramatically from floor level to several inches above the ankle.

■ ABOVE: Several "Good Time Girls" chartered this Pope-Toledo automobile for a drive under the midnight sun in Fairbanks on June 21, 1910. Notice the veils covering their hats to hold them in place while motoring. PHOTO COURTESY OF THE PIONEER MUSEUM, PM 1968.068.000.

8. MOTORING CLOTHING~

During the earliest days of the auto-mobile, drivers and passengers wore whatever outerwear they had available, usually the same attire they chose for riding in horse-drawn carriages. It was a messy affair, as many early automobiles lacked tops or windscreens.

As motoring increased in popularity after 1900, specialized clothing and other gear became essential to protect drivers and passengers from clouds of dust, mud, oil splatters, and flying rocks. Both men and women donned volumi-nous coats or dusters to keep their clothes clean. These were typically made from tan or ecru-colored fabrics, which hid dirt better than bright or dark colors. Most dusters had large pockets for maps, gloves, bandanas, and other travel necessities.

■ **LEFT: 1910s raw silk motoring duster trimmed with contrasting navy silk accents and silk-covered buttons.**
■ **ABOVE: Pongee silk motoring bonnet worn to protect hair from wind and dust.**

Male motorists wore caps, goggles, leather gauntlets, and dusters of linen, canvas, or oilskin that protected their clothes while changing flat tires and mak-ing on-the-spot repairs. Women favored silk or linen dusters, often decorated with pretty trimmings. They wrapped their fashionably large hats with scarves to hold them in place, and many wore gauze veils to protect their faces from dirt and oil. Linen bonnets also came into fashion and were favored by women who dared to drive their own car.

1915 Men's Fur Coat
Wrapped in a warm bear hug

To stay warm during cold winter months, motorists often wore fur coats and covered their laps with blankets. Alaska pioneers typically wore coats made from the fur of raccoon, beaver, or wolf. This coat, on loan from Rocky McDonald, was made from the hides of three black bears. The Russian-style hat was made from beaver fur.

On longer rides in Alaska, blankets made from bison, caribou, or moose provided extra insulation for passengers. Metal warmers filled with hot charcoal bricks helped keep their feet warm.

■ BELOW: Jack Ingram in a raccoon coat with his 'Ski-Dodge' in Chitina, ca. 1917. JOHN ZUG ALBUM 1980-68-198, ARCHIVES, UNIVERSITY OF ALASKA FAIRBANKS.

1910-1912 Duster Coats
Fashionable protection from wind and dirt

■ LEFT: ca. 1910 ¾-length ecru muslin motoring coat, embroidered with a silk floss wisteria floral design. Shown with a linen motoring bonnet.

■ RIGHT: 1910–1915 ecru pongee silk duster trimmed in cream open work lace and appliquéd mauve soutache. Pongee is a raw fiber gathered from the cocoons of wild silk moths. It was an important export to the U.S. from China in the early 1900s. The horsehair hat is trimmed with silk satin ribbon, rosebuds, and tulle veiling.

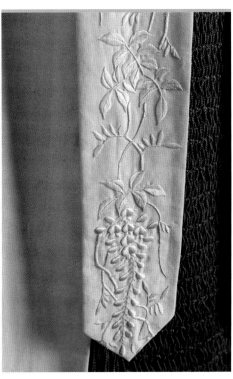

■ BELOW: 1912 Peerless touring car

■ **ABOVE: A woman wearing a hobble skirt sits on the dock in Douglas, across Gastineau Channel from Juneau.** ED ANDREWS PHOTOGRAPHS ASL-PCA-162, ALASKA STATE LIBRARY.

9. HOBBLED BY FASHION

Of all the fashions of the Edwardian era, the most restrictive was the hobble skirt. Popular between 1910 and 1913, these dresses were so narrow at their base that wearers were forced to walk with tiny, geisha-like steps. To keep from taking too long of a stride and ripping out the seams of their narrow skirts, some women wore a device called a hobble garter underneath. It consisted of a fabric band wrapped around their legs just below the knees.

Journalists denounced the hobble skirt as freakish and unsafe, and some employers banned them in the workplace. Others believed that a woman who could walk gracefully in a hobble skirt displayed sophistication, sensuality, and a hint of mirth. Ironically, these restrictive garments were popular at the same time suffragists were demanding more freedoms. Many of them wore these unusually challenging skirts while campaigning for the right to vote.

As women became more active, hobble skirts became less restricted with the addition of concealed slits, hidden pleats, draping, and sometimes even Turkish trousers. By 1914 the hobble skirt fad was on the way out, in part to accommodate the ever-increasing popularity of driving and riding in automobiles.

This ca. 1913 cobalt blue dress is made from a fine woven silk jacquard with oriental or early Art Deco motifs. The skirt is hobbled by a placket that hugs the knees, and the lower part of the dress is very narrow. The dress is trimmed with a black velvet sash and collar, silk-covered buttons, a lace modesty insert at the neck, and floral lace cuffs. Women often accessorized their hobble dresses and oriental-influenced tunics with feather-trimmed turbans and turban-style hats, such as the straw toque shown.

ca. 1914 Day Dress
Last days of the hobble skirt

This raw silk dress has a skirt that is full at the top and tapers at the bottom, similar to the less restrictive hobble skirts worn as this peculiar fashion faded. The elaborate, pin-striped bodice, ¾-length sleeves, and layered peplum are trimmed with silk, ivory net ruffles, and fabric-covered cord spirals.

ca. 1913 Evening Gown
A provocative and dangerous dress

The hobbled skirt on this sumptuous evening gown prevented the wearer from taking a normal stride or easily climbing stairs. Its ecru silk satin bodice and train are adorned with silver bugle beads and rhinestones. The V-neck is finished with a black chiffon flower decorated with beads and silver metallic trim. The narrow, ecru satin skirt has a black net overskirt decorated with crystal beads embroidered in a scroll and leaf pattern.

■ **Above:** Enjoying an afternoon outing in a Cadillac near Fairbanks around 1916. Hiatt Family Photographs 2009–0019-30, Archives, University of Alaska Fairbanks.

10. POST-EDWARDIAN FASHIONS

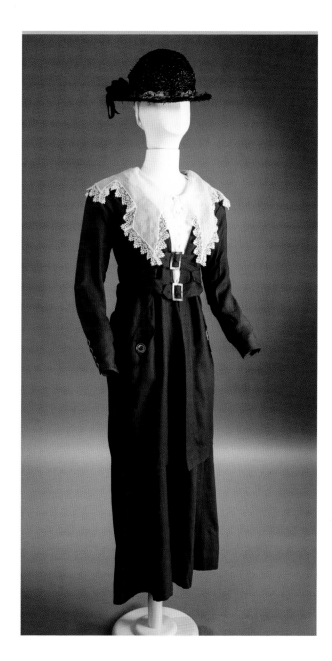

The First World War had a broad impact on fashion. As women began taking on wartime jobs, daywear became more practical. Shorter, fuller skirts and looser waists allowed for a greater range of movement. High, stiff collars were replaced by square and V-shaped necklines. Women discarded their corsets for two-piece undergarments consisting of a girdle with garters and the forerunner to the modern bra.

In 1915 a style of dress appeared called a war crinoline that featured a very full, bell-shaped skirt that required layers of petticoats. Hemlines rose to 8 inches from the floor, leading women to direct more attention to fashionable footwear. They wore their hair shorter or in chignons, and narrower hats became more practical for daywear and motoring about in automobiles.

Day dresses during the war were somber and monochrome, with dark and muted colors predominating. The tunic-and-skirt look was popular, as were suit jackets with large belts. Embellishments were mostly limited to large collars and cuffs, scarves, and military-inspired belts, buckles, braiding, and epaulettes.

In contrast, eveningwear retained a feminine flare with soft colors and decorations of lace, silk tulle, and artificial flowers.

By 1918 skirts narrowed again and hemlines began to fall. Clothing became more colorful and elaborate after the war ended, hinting at the spirited fashions to come in the 1920s.

■ **ABOVE: 1918 day dress made of cotton printed with floral and pebble swirls. The double skirt, square neckline, and shawl collar were popular on daywear during the Teens. A strip of lace at the neckline and bands of black velvet add flare to this otherwise understated dress.**

■ **LEFT: ca. 1915-1919 day dress, similar to the one in the photo on the opposite page. It is a very plain but tailored dress made of lightweight brown wool with a two-buckle, criss-cross belt.**

ca. 1915 Evening Dress
Vibrant color during a somber time

The rich garnet color of this silk evening gown was special for its time. During the war, fabric colors were typically muted or dark. Some people thought that pretty gowns like this one were a frivolous indulgence during a time of scarcity. Others felt that colorful dresses brought cheer during a sad time, likely the opinion of the lady who wore this gown.

Two layers of tulle decorated with satin rosebuds and silk floss embroidery overlay the sleeveless underdress of taffeta. The waist belt and bouquet of silk rosebuds on the bodice add charm to this delightful gown.

ca. 1916 Tea Dress
Fantastic feminine details

This ultra-feminine afternoon frock has an underdress made from lavender-dyed silk, overlain by cream cotton netting. The overhanging bodice, flared skirt, and elbow-length sleeves are decorated with ecru lace and extravagant embroidery. Lace inserts were sewn into both the front and surplice-style back of the bodice.

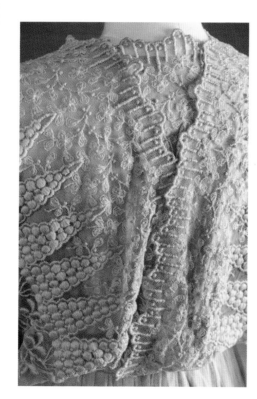

1915 Evening Coat
Ottoman-inspired couture

Jeanne Lanvin (1867-1946) was a French couturier and one of the first designers to use lamé. The House of Lanvin she founded is the oldest surviving fashion house in continuous existence. Lanvin loved to work with expensive fabrics and was known for her masterful embellishments of delicate trimmings, ruffles, appliqués, flowers, embroidery, and exquisite beadwork.

This rare and early Jeanne Lanvin brocade evening coat was exhibited in the French Pavilion of the 1915 Panama-Pacific International Exposition in San Francisco. It was also featured in a 1915 issue of *Vogue* magazine.

The coat is a wonderful example of Orientalism—Western fashion's incorporation of the loose silhouettes, brilliant colors, lush fabrics, and luminous patterns from Asia, Africa, and the Middle East. The brocade is infused with bronze thread, gold metallic lace, gold lamé, and silk rosettes. The gold lamé skirt of the coat is trimmed with gold lace and green ribbon rosettes.

The coat's loose fit was designed to cover the wide skirts that were popular in 1915. This, along with its large collar and bold fabrics, provided a preview of the showy coats that would sweep the fashion world in the 1920s.

1916-1917 Evening Dress
Precursor to Roaring 20s style

This silk gown exemplifies the style transition between the late Edwardian period and the 1920s. Its loose waist, asymmetrical draping, strap sleeves, and lavish beading hint at the showy flapper dresses yet to come. The dress is also an example of the new trend for wearing black in everyday fashion, rather than only for mourning. Its underdress of black silk is covered with black netting, livened up with blue net appliqué and cut steel beadwork.

■ LEFT: Evening purse with a cut steel fringe tassel, silver chain, and silver plate frame.

1915-1918 Day Dress
Simplicity with sweet trimmings

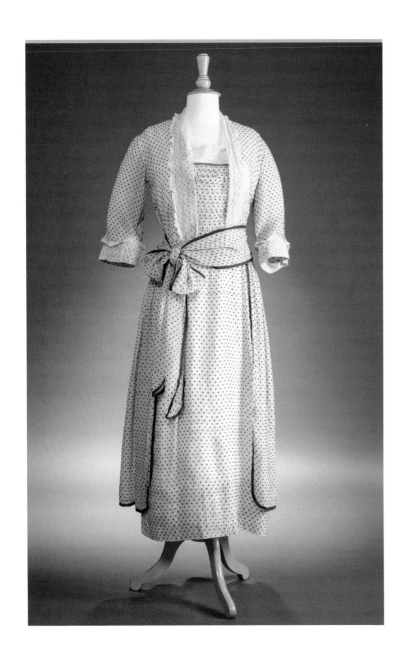

A wide sash, flying side panels, and lace on the sleeves, vestee, and shawl collar brighten this otherwise plain summer dress. The sheer beige and brown Swiss dot cotton print is further trimmed with brown piping.

■ **BELOW: 1918 Stutz Bulldog Special**

1917-1919 Evening Dress
Sequined flair for a night on the town

It's easy to imagine a wealthy lady wearing this couture dress and riding to a fancy dinner in the stylish Biddle town car shown below.

Like the Biddle, this dress embodies quality workmanship and high style. The tight rows of sequins on the silk netting overlaying the silk underdress were carefully applied by hand. Stripes of sequins adorn the sleeves, skirt sides, and hem, and the heavily sequined outer layer of the bodice further enhances the beauty of the dress. Small lead weights were sewn into both the skirt hem and portions of the bodice overlay so each would hang properly.

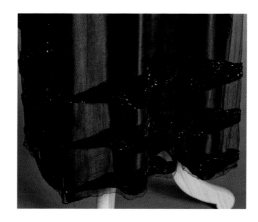

■ **LEFT: Fountainhead Antique Auto Museum manager Willard Vinton with a 1918 Biddle Town Car.**

ca. 1916-1917 Evening Dress
Gold on gold glamour

As the Teens progressed, sleeveless evening gowns with contrasting sashes came into fashion. The fabric on this dazzling dress is gold metallic brocade with a raised foliate pattern. The bolero-like bodice, peplum, and sash are made of gold lamé lace with silk floral highlights. The deep V-neck features a modesty panel of gold net and embroidery. The ensemble includes gold brocade shoes with gold leather strap work.

1918-1919 Evening Wrap
Cocooned against the evening chill

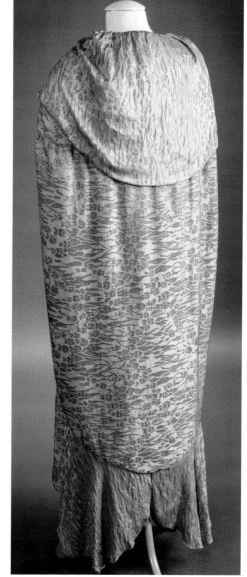

Cloaks draped over bare shoulders provided a sensible and stylish cover for sleeveless evening dresses. This cloak is made from gold lamé silk brocade with apricot silk lining. Its shoulder yoke extends back into a loose hood. The lapels drape into waves of loose ruffles that cascade down to a deep flounce wrapped around the bottom of the cloak. It is a fine example of an early cocoon-style coat, which had wide shoulders and narrowed toward the hem.

11. 1920s FASHIONS

Fashion in the 1920s was greatly influenced by women's changing roles in society. Public acceptance of jobs for young, unmarried ladies increased, women gained the right to vote, and more of them drove automobiles. A new sense of freedom and self-expression took hold, exemplified through carefree fashions and exuberant lifestyles.

In the early 1920s, dresses became more practical for work as well as play. The new ideal shape became slender and boyish, with no curves and a flat chest. It was the antithesis of the matronly silhouette of the Edwardian era.

The chemise dress with short or no sleeves was a favorite style. Skirt hems had dropped back down to lower-calf length in the late Teens, but were now fashioned with pleats, gathers, or slits to allow motion. Waistlines dropped to the hips, or disappeared completely.

Cloches were popular throughout the 1920s, and women bobbed or cut their hair short to fit under these radical, bell-shaped hats. Many wore their cloches so low on their foreheads they had to lift their chins to see forward.

The mid-1920s saw the arrival of the flapper—the rebellious, pleasure-seeking girl who dashed about in her automobile by day and danced away the night. Flapper dresses were boxy and hung straight from the shoulders. Despite their boyish shape, they were stylish, feminine, and often quite ornate.

Between 1926 and 1928, hemlines reached the knees for the first time, then dropped back down in 1929. As the decade ended, natural curves in the silhouette began reappearing, as dresses began reclaiming the feminine form.

■ LEFT: 1926-1928 day dress, with lace and silk chiffon layered over a pink rayon underdress.

■ RIGHT: 1924-1927 black crepe de chine dress decorated with a large parrot worked in colorful beads and metallic gold thread.

■ ABOVE: A group of students at the Alaska Agricultural College and School of Mines in Fairbanks show off their 1920s style. UNIVERSITY OF ALASKA GENERAL FILE 1958-1026-65, ARCHIVES, UNIVERSITY OF ALASKA FAIRBANKS.

ca. 1922-1923 Evening Dress
Ornamentation inspired by Egypt

Although the fashion world had embraced the exotic designs and fabrics of the Middle East several years prior, the discovery of King Tutankhamen's tomb in 1922 set off a firestorm of "Egyptomania." Dresses like this one incorporated the graphic designs found on Egyptian artifacts, such as trapezoids, zigzags, geometric shapes, and sunbursts. This frock is made of gold lamé and is heavily decorated with glass beads and seed pearls. A beaded flower with tassels sits low on the left hip.

■ ABOVE: Evening purse decorated in gold and silver beads.

1921-1922 Evening Dress

A beautifully embellished "little black dress"

1925 Evening Dress and Coat

An ensemble trimmed in fiery brilliance

■ LEFT and above: A negative daisy pattern outlined in blue beads is surrounded by swirls of black beads on the sheer bodice, sleeves, and skirt of this silk chiffon shift. The matching tie belt could be worn at or below the natural waist.

■ RIGHT: Paste is a very heavy and transparent leaded glass that simulates the fire and brilliance of gemstones. This black silk shift and matching jacket are beautifully trimmed with paste rhinestones, gold lamé embroidery, and cut glass beads.

1925-1929 Work Dress

Sensible but stylish office wear

Rayon, a semi-synthetic fiber made from the cellulose of wood or cotton pulp, exploded in popularity in the 1920s. Also known as artificial silk, it was the first manufactured fiber used in the clothing industry. A related but chemically different fabric called acetate (or rayon acetate) was made by adding acetic acid to cellulose.

Fabrics made from acetate, rayon, and rayon blends draped beautifully and were much more affordable than silk. The versatile fibers could be made into taffeta, charmeuse, crepe, organza, or lush velvets.

■ RIGHT: Navy rayon or acetate dress with pink inset bib collar covered with lace. The right shoulder is trimmed with a pink bow and streamer, and pink lining peeks through the eye-catching flares at mid-sleeve.

■ LEFT: This navy rayon or acetate dress with long, fitted sleeves and a pleated skirt is an example of the conservative attire working women wore during the 1920s. Though straight and curveless, the red trim and inset ivory silk at the neckline and collar add personality to the dress.

Late 1920s Day Dress

Striking pink accents on navy

ca. 1925 Day Dress

A cheerful chemise for a garden party

The most popular party to attend or host in the summer was an outdoor tea or garden party. Women preferred short-sleeved cotton dresses for these gatherings, which they accessorized with a hat, white shoes, and sheer stockings in nude, white, or a pastel shade similar to their dress.

Wide panels of intricate cutwork embroidery highlight the sleeves, front, and back of this sweet cotton lawn dress. Side ties loosely define its low waist.

■ **LEFT: Wide-brimmed horsehair hat trimmed with ochre velvet.**

ca. 1922 Tabard

Style lifted from the Middle Ages

A chic cut for evening dresses in the 1920s was the straight tabard. It consisted of long fabric panels in front and back, linked by side belts, cords, or straps. The tabard was based on the decorated, open-sided smocks worn by knights during the Middle Ages. It could be worn over a dress, slip, or pants.

Italian fashion and textile designer Maria Monaci Gallenga was famous for her metallic printed costumes and medieval-inspired designs. She and her husband developed a unique printing process using a mixture of brass, copper, and zinc pigments painted or block printed onto fabrics.

Gallenga created this trained, black velvet tabard, which is covered with silver stenciled mythological creatures and arabesque patterns. The front and back panels are connected by cord ties decorated with Murano beads, and elegant black chiffon side streamers attached at the shoulders.

■ **ABOVE: ca. 1920s black satin embroidered t-strap shoes.**

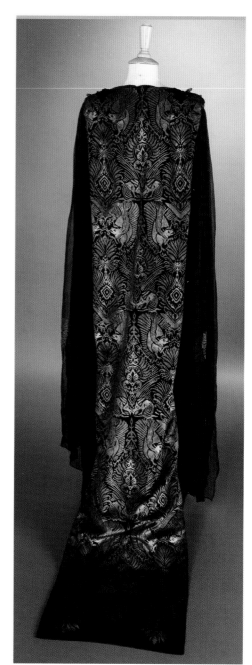

1923-1925 Evening Dress
A jewel of a gown

This sleeveless, silk velvet dress offered a striking vision of the enchanting flapper fashions about to burst onto the scene. The loose, low waist, low décolletage, asymmetrical hem, and beautiful embellishments foreshadowed the high-spirited glamour that would soon sweep the fashion world.

The ornamentation around the scoop neck and armholes consists of prong-set paste jewels on ivory chiffon. There is also a paste ornament set in the large ruched velvet rosette adorned with tassels on the drop waist. The silk charmeuse underdress is edged in chiffon. Together, these details created a lush, sensuous gown that would have flattered any wearer.

■ **LEFT:** Woven silk evening purse with intricate floral embroidery, seed pearl trim, and a gilt frame.

83

1928-1929 Wedding Dress
A treasured heirloom

During the 1920s, long, heavy bridal gowns were replaced by lighter and shorter lace and silk dresses that mirrored the current fashions. Women typically accessorized their wedding dresses with a cloche, headband, or long veil attached to a tiara.

The bodice of ivory silk satin on this dress has the appearance of a low-cut jacket, gathered by ruching in the front to define the waist. It is accented by a lace yoke and deep hip drapes with bows on the low points. The asymmetrical hem was common in the late 1920s.

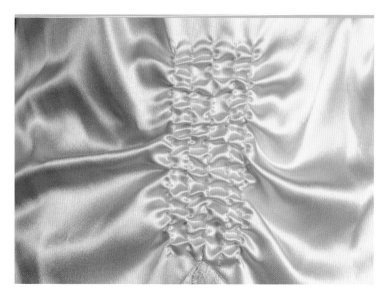

■ ABOVE: Kid leather wedding shoes with silk bows and Louis heels.

1928-1930 Day Dress
A return to femininity

In 1928, waistlines began to reappear and hemlines began dropping. The most fashionable hemlines hung slightly below the knees in front and trailed lower in back, as on this dress. Its silk fabric and matching belt are printed with gold, ivory, and red florals on a navy background. The wide collar and droopy bow were common accents for the time.

The ensemble includes lace gloves, a vintage-inspired necklace, and navy straw cloche trimmed with yellow and ivory flowers.

■ LEFT: Marvel and Lillian Crosson show off the shorter dresses that were popular during the Roaring 20s. Lillian's dress has a Peter Pan collar and Marvel's has an asymmetrical hem. CROSSON FAMILY PAPERS 2006-103-161, ARCHIVES, UNIVERSITY OF ALASKA FAIRBANKS. ■ RIGHT: A young woman poses on stage in a taffeta dress and headband. ALBERT JOHNSON PHOTOGRAPH COLLECTION 1989-166-354, ARCHIVES, UNIVERSITY OF ALASKA FAIRBANKS.

12. FLAPPER DRESSES

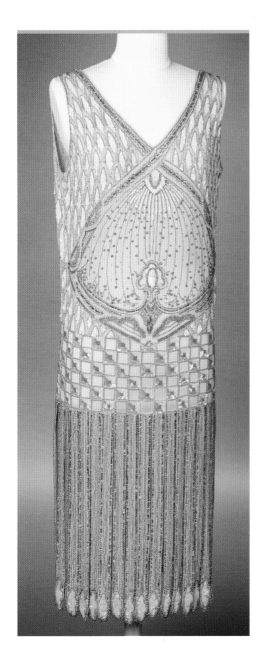

The ultimate evening dress during the flapper era was the layered chemise, lavishly embellished with beads, sequins, embroidery, lace and/or fringe sewn onto a net tunic worn over a colorful underdress. Most were sleeveless and some had shockingly low backs.

These dresses were accessorized with beaded purses, Mary Jane or t-strap shoes, stockings, and feathered headbands, decorative hairpieces, or beaded skullcaps. Many dresses, skullcaps, and purses carried patterns of Art Deco geometrics or Egyptian-inspired designs.

The best dresses were made in France, where professional beaders attached sequins and glass beads by hand using a technique called tambour beading. The tambour process entailed making a chain stitch with a crochet hook, essentially combining embroidery and crochet techniques. It allowed beads to be applied much faster than traditional hand sewing.

A beaded chemise could weigh several lbs., which makes their care and display in museums somewhat challenging.

■ **BELOW: 1927 Stutz Black Hawk speedster**

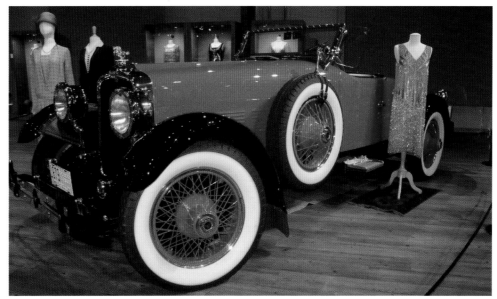

■ **LEFT: ca. 1926 ivory silk crepe flapper dress** attributed to French fashion designer Jean Patou. The dress is decorated with Art Deco motifs in peach, green, white, and gold glass beads and sequins. The long, narrow beaded flaps at the bottom created dramatic movement as the wearer danced away the night.
■ **ABOVE: Aviator-style beaded flapper cap** with chinstrap. Made of gold lace with appliqué curlicues and a triangle front. Studded with rhinestone diamonds and seed pearls.

1925-1926 Evening Dress
Evocative of shimmering Northern Lights

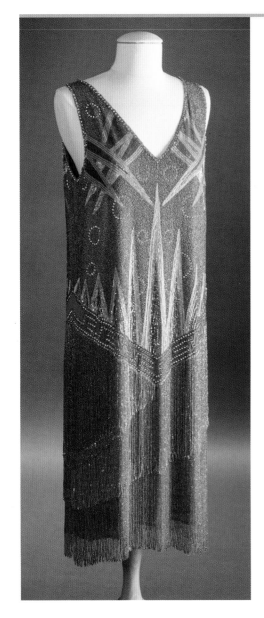

By 1925, many evening dresses were designed to accentuate the wild movements of the Charleston and jazz dancing. Made from pale lavender chiffon, this sleeveless dress is trimmed with sparkling silver sequins, hand set rhinestones, and periwinkle beads in a sumptuous Art Deco design. Whenever its wearer moved, the asymmetrical, fringed tiers must have danced and shimmered like the magical Aurora Borealis.

■ **LEFT: 1920s silk brocade evening shoes with gilt leather strap work.**

1925 Evening Dress
Haute couture in coral silk

Exquisite craftsmanship is evident on this coral silk crepe evening gown. The V-neck and armholes are decorated with a band of red and spruce bugle beads and pearls, while the lower half of the shift has arabesque patterns of cartouches, arches, and scrolls in pearls and gold, spruce, red and white beads. There is no label on the chemise, but it resembles a very similar dress from the Paris fashion house of British designer Edward Molyneux. Known as "the designer to whom a fashionable woman would turn if she wanted to be absolutely right without being utterly predictable," Molyneux was a favorite among actresses including Greta Garbo and Marlene Dietrich.

■ **ABOVE: Art Deco skullcap with trim made from gold bullion metallic thread, and accents of soutache designs and beaded sequins.**

■ **LEFT: Enameled metal mesh purse by Mandalian with Art Noveau iris designs, V-bottom, chain fringe, and a metal carry chain, embossed clasp, and frame.**

ca. 1926 Evening Dress

Featured on Antiques Roadshow

ca. 1926 Evening Dress

A sapphire on the dance floor

■ LEFT: This flapper dress from a New York estate appeared on a 2010 episode of the "Antiques Roadshow" television program. Made from periwinkle silk chiffon and beige crepe, the shift is heavily embellished with a mix of French and Art Deco designs. Its silver fleur-de-lis patterns are surrounded by harlequin diamonds of gold sequins. The elongated scalloped fringe created exaggerated movement when the wearer hit the dance floor.

■ RIGHT: This blue chiffon party dress is completely covered in vertical rows of cobalt sequins. A cut steel hip buckle and velvet bow adorn the right hip.

ca. 1926 Evening Dress

A sequined bouquet of roses

A flapper's dream, this French-made dance chemise (and our cover dress) is the epitome of 1920s fashion and frivolity. The heavily embellished shift is covered in swaths of opalescent sequins, stripes of gray and black sequins, and large, pink beaded Deco roses. A three-dimensional flower made of silver and pink sequins rests on the left shoulder. The hemline sits at the knees, which was the highest hemlines would go in the 1920s.

■ **ABOVE: ca. 1915-1920 silver lamé floral brocade shoes with single button straps. This style of footwear was popular throughout the 1920s, especially for dancing.**

1926–1928 Evening Dress
Heavy French couture

Almost every inch of the silk netting of this chemise is covered in silver beads and gelatin sequins. This makes it surprisingly heavy—nearly 5 lbs. (2.3 kg). The tambour-beaded overskirt with side slits attaches at the dropped waistline and features rows of fish scale scallops. The only areas of the netting not covered are the centers of the scallops at the waist, hem, and center front.

The dress still bears its original label, "Made in France by Frenchshire, Paris." The weight of the dress no doubt created fascinating movement, and its thousands of beads and sequins must have glittered to rival the stars in the night sky.

■ **ABOVE:** Mandalian enamel mesh purse with an Art Deco design and Van Dyke fringe. The silver frame is embossed with a fleur-de-lis and scrollwork.
■ **RIGHT:** Late 1920s ivory satin d'Orsay (open-sided) t-strap shoes with decorative cutouts on the vamps.

1926-1928 Evening Dress
Black velvet sophistication

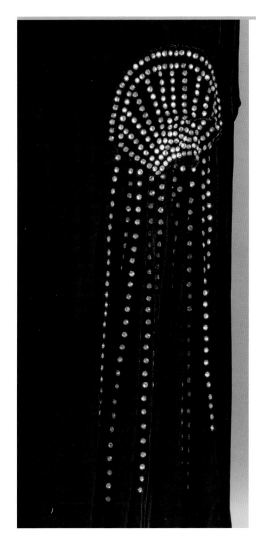

S o much more than the "little black dress" made famous by Coco
Chanel! This otherwise simple black velvet evening gown has a
sparkling sunburst and shell design made from rhinestones at one
shoulder and hip.

■ Rɪɢʜᴛ: This crocheted miser's purse has
a short slit in the narrow midsection for
dropping coins into the different ends. The two
rings could be moved to close off the purse's
ends to secure their contents.

ca. 1928-1929 Evening Dress

With a sassy " hanky hem"

The handkerchief hem on this sleeveless evening dress pulled the focus away from the hips and elongated the lower half of the body. It also made the dress appear long while the wearer stood still, but flashed a lot of leg when she sat or danced.

The black netting on this dress is trimmed in vertical rows of black sequins and large flowers of jewel-toned sequins. Black tulle streamers of different lengths trail from each hip.

■ **Above: ca. 1914–1917 silk brocade tango boots with gold scrollwork, criss-cross laces, and leather vamps. Tango boots were popular during the dance craze that extended from 1910 through the 1920s.**

1929 Evening Dress
Emerald and silver shimmers on ebony

The two tiers of this gown are covered in black bugle beads, except for the tulle hems. The left side of the gown carries a design of cascading leaves made from green and silver beads and green pastes. The gown may be a Jeanne Lanvin creation, as it closely resembles a similar 1929 dress made by this famous French designer.

■ **Above top: Skullcap beaded on a net base with partial gold lamé lining. Cording of silk and metallic thread further accent the beading and fill areas.**

■ **Above: 1920s black satin d'Orsay style shoes with decorative rhinestone straps and trim.**

13. ROBES DE STYLE

Not every lady could, or wanted to, mold their curves to fit the flat chest and narrow hips of the boyish 1920s silhouette. For curvy women or those who simply preferred a more feminine look, an alternative style consistently present throughout the decade was the Robe de Style (pronounced steel). It was a signature design of French couturier Jeanne Lanvin.

Inspired by the exaggerated, wide-hipped court dresses of the 18th century, the Robe de Style, also known as a picture dress or basque dress, was primarily for eveningwear. In stark contrast to straight chemises, Robes de Style had snug bodices, defined waists, and long, bouffant skirts that jutted out at the hips. Some of the skirts were so full that they required side petticoats, panniers, or hoops worn underneath.

Ranging in length from just below the knee to the ankle, the gowns were typically made from luxurious fabrics like silk taffeta, organdy, velvet, chiffon, or satin. More subdued fullness in the skirt could be created through gathering, pleating, and shirring; however, many styles required support from pannier-like underpinnings.

■ THIS PAGE: ca. 1925 Robe de Style of black silk tissue taffeta trimmed with ivory embroidered chiffon at the collar and sleeves. The skirt, accented with shirring, has fullness supported by integral wire panniers. The waistband culminates in a large bow in back, and is decorated in front with a colorful, jewel-toned velvet floral appliqué.

■ LEFT: Late 1920s black satin Mary Jane shoes with gold trim.

1923 Robe de Style

A romantic alternative to the straight chemise

During the early 1920s, the waist placement on Robes de Style was natural, with the close-fitting, short-sleeved bodice having a scooped or boat neckline. As the decade progressed, variations of the Robe de Style appeared, including ones with a sleeveless, deep-V neck bodice and dropped waistline.

In keeping with the flash and luxury idolized by Roaring 20s fashion, the gowns could be lavishly trimmed in glitzy beads, sequins, lamé, diamante, and paste.

This Robe de Style features gray-green silk gauze adorned with variegated velvet stripes, metallic ribbon, and a front lace panel flanked by bands decorated with cloth flowers, metallic ribbon, and lace. The cap sleeve bodice has an inset made from silver metallic lace over tulle. A built-in wire structure shaped like a basket extends the hips.

14. 1920s EVENING COATS AND WRAPS

A stylish flapper didn't just wear a coat for warmth. With its slouchy, casual cut and luxe fabrics, her coat proclaimed ease, wealth, and opulence. Often tailored to match a specific dress, flappers combined their coats with cloche hats, beads, make-up cases, cigarette holders, and other accessories to create a look equal to a stunning work of art.

Evening coats during the 1920s were colorful and generally calf length, with the wrap style being most favored. Shawls were also a popular cover for sleeveless dresses. Many coats, wraps, and shawls featured elaborate beading, fringe, and motifs inspired by the styles of the Orient and Egypt. Oversize collars on winter coats were often trimmed in fur or silk fringe.

■ **ABOVE:** Silk and gold lamé evening wrap with hood. Printed with lush rose motifs.

■ **ABOVE:** 1928 Oakland All-American landau sedan

■ **RIGHT:** Silk brocade piano shawl with hand-knotted silk fringe. Piano shawls were originally used to decorate and protect the surface of grand pianos, but were incorporated into women's fashion in the late Teens.

■ **Above:** Lillian Crosson (left) and a friend sit near the Copper River where it passes by Childs Glacier. Crosson Family Papers 2006-103-40, Archives, University of Alaska Fairbanks.

ca. 1925 Evening Jacket
A palette of Chinese motifs

An extraordinary amount of handcrafted embellishment covers this chinoiserie jacket attributed to Parisian designer Jeanne Margaine-Lacroix. Margaine-Lacroix was known for the revolutionary corsetless dresses she introduced in 1908, and for her later garments lavishly embellished with Chinese and Egyptian Revival themed motifs. This gold lamé jacket is covered with fine details, including pagodas and human figures hand stitched in silk, beads, and sequins.

■ LEFT: Art Deco dance purse from the 1920s made from black celluloid with rhinestone trim. One side of the small purse contains a rectangular mirror. The other side has separate compartments for powder and coins.

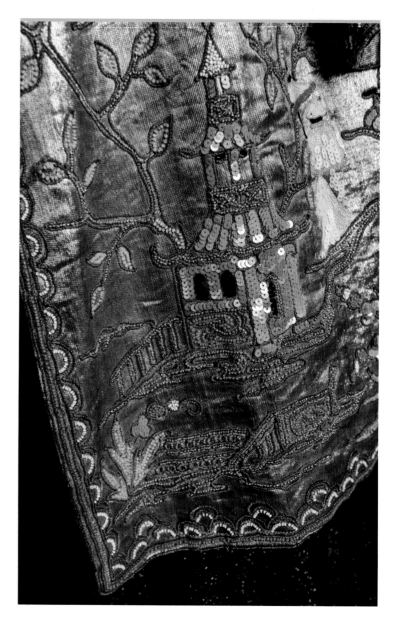

ca. 1925 Evening Coat
Wrapped in lush velvet and lamé

Wraps were also known as clutch coats because the wearer had to hold one closed by clutching the sides together with her hand. The lack of a clasp allowed the wrap to fall open and stylishly reveal the dress underneath.

Woven with metallic threads, this multi-colored, gold lamé coat features the columnar silhouette that was popular during the 1920s. It has kimono-style sleeves and is trimmed in lush, rust-colored velvet.

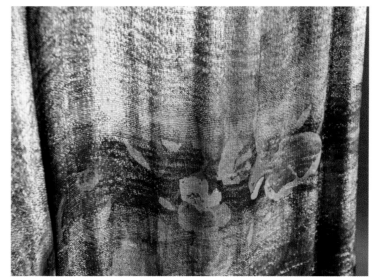

1925–1928 Evening Coat
Dramatic ruching and roses

The most sumptuous chestnut silk velvet pairs with opulent gold lamé on this Art Deco reversible coat. Its rich details include large roses, brilliant colors, and an exotic-looking fringed silk trim that mimics monkey fur, a popular embellishment of the time. The print was inspired by the stylized roses of Paul Poiret, a leading French couturier known for his bold, Neoclassical and Orientalist fashions.

Worn lamé side out, the two oversized ruched velvet roses at the collar echo the orange roses in the lamé. The same orange roses were cut out and appliquéd at the back hem of the coat, embellished with gold braid and sequins.

Reversed, the coat is more understated, with an Art Deco flavor created by geometric bands of gold lamé against the soft chestnut velvet. To create interest, the velvet of the coat's body was woven in a shadow stripe to contrast with matching, plain-woven chestnut velvet at the hem and sleeves.

The ca. 1920s hat shown is made of orange silk. It has a pleated crown and is trimmed with a rhinestone pin and dyed ostrich feather. The shoes below are ca. 1920s black satin ankle-straps with D-shaped cutwork.

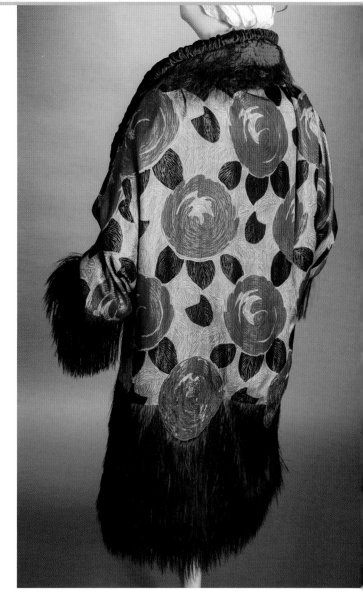

■ Right: 1925
Stutz Speedway
Six sportbrohm

ca. 1925 Opera Coat
Beetle mania meets fashion

For centuries, people from locales such as India, Thailand, Australia, Central America, the West Indies, and ancient Egypt used metallic wood-boring beetles for personal adornment. In the nineteenth century, these iridescent "jewel beetles" winged their way into European fashion.

Women in Victorian England loved to wear dresses, shawls, and fans embellished with glittering touches of the exotic from the Empire's far-flung lands. In addition to adorning their hats with beautiful feathers and even whole birds from other countries, many women wore jewelry that incorporated entire jewel beetles. Victorian ladies on the cutting edge of fashion even wore live jewel beetles tethered to their clothing by tiny golden chains, or decorated their hairdos with live fireflies!

Often, just the hard, chitonous wing cases from beetles were sewn onto textiles. Called elytra, the hard cases protect a beetle's fragile flight wings and also provide aerodynamic lift when held open. These elytra were—and still are—harvested by the millions in the hardwood forests of Burma after the beetles swarm, mate, and die.

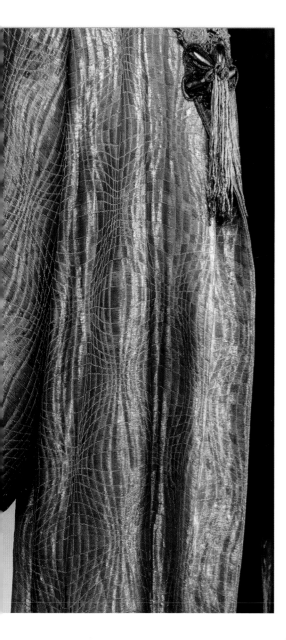

The brilliant metallic coloration in the elytra sewn onto this coat is not from pigment, but instead is caused by the microscopic texture of the beetles' exoskeletons. The iridescence of beetle elytra is not easily replicated, and their seemingly magical coloration explains our centuries-old fascination with this most unusual natural jewel.

15. FORTUNY DELPHOS GOWNS

S panish artist and designer Mariano Fortuny was renowned for his legendary textiles, which were wildly popular for their beauty and versatility. Around 1907 he debuted what became his best known and most admired garment, the simple yet elegant Delphos dress. Drawing inspiration from the pleated linen chitons of ancient Greece, Delphos gowns were made of fine, mushroom-pleated silk that "clung to the form in long, crinkled lines and shimmered like the skin of a snake." The dresses hung freely from the shoulders and molded gracefully to the wearers' bodies.

The Delphos dresses came in only one size and were meant to be worn without elaborate underwear. Originally intended as tea gowns for informal entertaining at home, by the 1920s it became acceptable, albeit risqué, to wear a Fortuny gown out as evening attire.

No two of Fortuny's gowns were alike, as each one was individually handcrafted in his Venice studio. The color of each fabric was built up in layers like a painting, with the

satin-weaved silks dipped in natural dyes up to 15 times to enrich the color. Fortuny never used the identical design or color combination on any two pieces of fabric.

■ THIS PAGE: ca. 1920 Fortuny Delphos gown of champagne-colored pleated silk with a hand-painted empire waistband. The armholes and side seams are decorated with white, blue, and yellow Murano glass beads.

Each of the four or five silk panels in a Fortuny gown contained up to 450 supple, accordion-like pleats, created on porcelain rollers. To help maintain the pleats, the dresses were rolled up and stored in small hatboxes. When an owner needed her gown cleaned, she sent it back to Venice because the pleats had to be reset.

Fortuny stitched hand-blown Venetian glass beads to the side seams of his dresses. The delicate beads helped weigh down the extremely lightweight fabric and pull it closer to the body.

A Fortuny gown was expensive, costing approximately $125 when an average tailor-made suit cost $10. Fortuny produced his Delphos gowns relatively unchanged for 40 years, keeping his pleating technique a carefully guarded secret during his lifetime. It has never been successfully duplicated since.

■ RIGHT: ca. 1930 Fortuny Delphos gown in a soft peach pleated silk with a scoop neckline, cap sleeves, hand-stenciled sash, and Murano glass beads of brown and white.

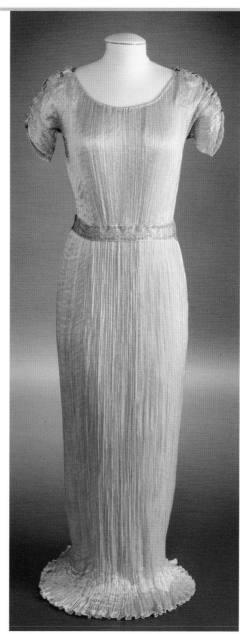

■ Aʙᴏᴠᴇ: **An auto party stops for a break in "The Gap" in Thompson Pass north of Valdez.** Oᴡᴇɴ Mᴇᴀʟꜱ Cᴏʟʟᴇᴄᴛɪᴏɴ 1987-007-0602, Vᴀʟᴅᴇᴢ Mᴜꜱᴇᴜᴍ.

16. 1930s FASHIONS

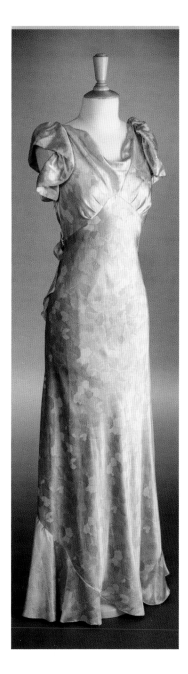

F ashion in the 1930s was driven by two disparate influences: the Great Depression and Hollywood. Most women could not afford expensive party frocks or multiple changes of dress throughout the day. They sewed more of their own clothing, and many copied styles worn by movie stars both on and off the silver screen. Department stores also offered replicas of Hollywood fashions in washable, easy-care fabrics.

By 1930, the fashionable silhouette had changed from the boyish, flapper look to a softer, more feminine shape. Waistlines re-appeared, breasts were lifted and separated for the first time, and hemlines dropped back to the bottom of the calf. By 1933 many dresses and suits emphasized the shoulders with pads, full collars, and butterfly or large, puffy sleeves.

Dresses now draped gracefully from the body's curves, thanks to a new way of cutting fabric "on the bias." By cutting diagonally against the grain of the threads rather than perpendicular to them, the fabric fell in a smooth vertical drape that clung flirtatiously to a woman's figure.

Daywear was ladylike, with skirts hugging the hips and thighs and then flaring at the hemline. Women loved fabrics with bold, floral prints. Longer gowns came back in vogue for eveningwear, greatly inspired by glamorous Hollywood actresses. The bared back was the new erotic zone, replacing the legs of the 1920s. Gowns were either

■ ABOVE: ca. 1930 blue straw cloche covered in gray-blue iridescent silk. Decorated with orange and gold silk feather-shaped appliqués.

sleeveless and worn with elbow-length gloves, or had full, cape-like, or puffed sleeves.

Shoes were available in many styles. Rounded or peep-toes with wide, thick heels were popular, as were pumps, flats, ankle straps, lace ups, spectators, and two tones. Hats came in a variety of styles, including berets, pillboxes, turbans, wide-brimmed, and ones with narrow, turned-up brims worn at rakish angles.

■ ABOVE: 1931–1932 rayon crepe floral print day dress with an asymmetrical hem and flutter sleeves. On loan from the Pioneers of Alaska, Women's Igloo #8.

ca. 1930-1931 Afternoon Dress
A cheerful chiffon butterfly

During the Depression, women wore housedresses for doing chores or lounging. Many farm women sewed their own housedresses from flour and feed sacks. Those women less affected by the economic downturn wore flirty, form-fitting frocks like this one to afternoon teas, luncheons, church, and other gatherings.

This sheer, silk chiffon dress has a sublime rose garden print of pink, gray, and green on a sunny buttercup background. The bias-cut skirt has floating panels and an irregular hem that make the dress drape beautifully. The butterfly sleeves, scoop collar, and belted waist were common features on dressy daywear during this era.

■ LEFT: 1933 Hupmobile Series K-321 Victoria

110

ca. 1935 Afternoon Dress

Feminine, form-fitting frills

Perfect for a summer lawn party! From the delicate floral print to the matching fabric flower on the scoop neck, this bias-cut silk dress epitomizes 1930s femininity. The horizontal pleats and rhinestone buckle on the self-fabric belt emphasize the narrow waist, while the softly pleated skirt drapes gracefully to the asymmetrical, ruffled hem.

■ **ABOVE:** ca. 1930 hat made of fine straw with silk floral decorations and brown ribbon along the brim and crown.

1931-1933 Summer Gown

Sheer ruffles and flounces

This sheer gown is made from a lightweight fabric named after Georgette de la Plante, an early twentieth century French dressmaker. The threads used in georgette fabric are highly twisted, which causes them to crinkle as they relax. This makes the fabric feel slightly rough, but also gives it a bouncy, flowing look.

This pale blue georgette gown is embroidered with blue and pink flowers. The ruffled collar, slit peek-a-boo back, puff sleeves, and pale blue corsage combine to make this an ultra-feminine and flirty dress.

■ ABOVE: ca. 1940s silk satin D'Orsay shoes with ankle straps, peep toes, and Spanish heels. Peep-toe heels made their first appearance in the late 1930s but didn't become widely popular until the 1940s.

■ RIGHT 1932 Cadillac V-16 Imperial limousine

ca. 1933 Evening Gown
Timeless style in fine lace

This delicate, sheer-netted gown shows the long, sleek look that was chic in the 1930s. It is made from rose-colored lace accented with gold lamé thread. Additional details on the gown include a cowl neckline, tapered waist, softly pleated skirt, and flutter sleeves.

■ RIGHT: ca. 1930 evening purse with silk floral embroidery on a gold lamé field.

■ LEFT: 1930 Packard 745 roadster

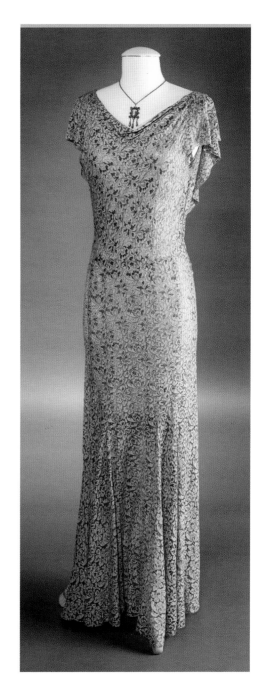

113

1936 Evening Dress
Cinematic glamour in rich velvet

Hollywood style is evident in this stunning ensemble, from the bias-cut gown's garnet silk velvet fabric and voluminous bishop sleeves, to its shirred neckline and matching turban. The inverted, circular empire waist accentuated the willowy silhouette so popular in the 1930s. Its matching belt with a rhinestone clasp drew further attention to the narrow waist. It is shown with a reproduction necklace.

■ BELOW: ca. 1920s Mary Jane shoes in lilac satin with Cuban heels.

1931-1934 Evening Gown

A striking contrast in black and gold

This beautifully tailored gown shimmers with eye-catching accents. The sleeves have exquisite golden bead and sequined details that provide dramatic contrast to the black silk dress. A matching black velvet and gold-toned metal mesh belt set with brilliant topaz pastes adds definition to the waistline.

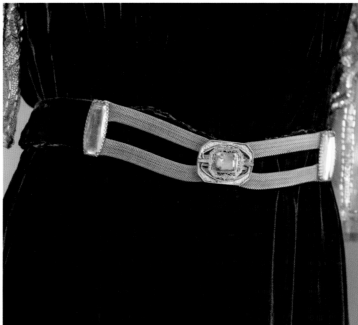

■ UPPER LEFT: ca. 1930 cut steel and metallic bead purse, with a gold-toned frame, chain, and interlocking beaded fringe.

■ LEFT: Black satin pumps with gold and silver leather straps and gold Cuban heels.

ca. 1937 Evening Ensemble
Simple but stunning

This simple, black velvet evening gown is made luminescent by the shimmering capelet encrusted with blue sequins and beads. The capelet is further adorned with a beaded fringe and Art Deco clasp.

■ ABOVE: Beaded purses remained popular through the 1930s. This ca. 1920s beaded velvet dance purse is covered in an Art Deco pattern of red, blue, and silver glass beads. A beaded wristlet is attached to the filigreed clasp.

ca. 1936 Evening Gown
Floral silk sophistication

This silk charmeuse gown shows how bias-cut fabric hugged and flattered a woman's figure. The center-gathered, low cowl bodice shows off the curved empire waist, while the flutter sleeves draw attention to the shoulders. Sumptuous ruffles, fabric poppies, and a low peplum accent the back of the dress. The skirt hugs the hips and then flares elegantly to a flounced hem that brushes the floor.

ca. 1938 Evening Ensemble
Lustrous damask for an elegant night out

Evening gowns with matching jackets were popular in the late 1930s. Women wore these ensembles to the theatre, nightclubs, and elegant restaurants. This gold-stenciled damask satin gown has a bias cut and spaghetti straps. The matching jacket features a stylish shawl collar with top stitching detail, leg o' mutton sleeves, and mink fur trim encircling the long hem.

1936-1937 Evening Gown

Fine lace in a frontier town

A popular formal dress style in the late 1930s was the empire-waisted gown with a large bow or fabric flower in the back. This one has a meandering floral pattern of white tambour lace contrasting with the black acetate dress underneath. Tambour lace was made by stretching a fine, machine-made net over a frame, and then embroidering the net with a fine hook to create a chain stitch. The elegant, crossover bodice on this dress features a deep V-neck adorned with a paste ornament, and a capelet-style collar that wraps around to a ruffled, plunging back. A self-fabric bow draws further attention to the exposed back. The skirt is gored to flare from the knees.

This dress belonged to a Fairbanks resident and is on loan from the Pioneers of Alaska.

1937-1940 Evening Gown
Hollywood-inspired glamour

The classic movie star look is embodied in this high-necked evening gown with its long, leg o' mutton sleeves and deep V-back that reaches almost to the waist. The bias-cut, silk velvet dress is trimmed with turquoise and bronze beads and turquoise sequins at the neckline, back, and wrists. While the high neck covers the cleavage, the low-cut back shows off the part of a woman's body that was considered an erogenous zone in the 1930s.

BELOW: 1936 Packard dual-windshield touring car

ca. 1938-1940 Evening Gown
Finery for a Fairbanks ball

When Alaska pioneers dressed up, it was often for a mid-winter ball. The Fairbanks lady who wore this gown no doubt drew admiring glances on the dance floor. It has a sheer, outer layer of chocolate brown netting with short, puff sleeves. The dainty shirt collar, front button closures, and striped bands of satin match the spaghetti-strap silk underdress. This elegant gown is generously on loan from the Pioneers of Alaska.

■ ABOVE: Children from St. Matthews Sunday School in Fairbanks gather with their Lenten offering cans for a photo on the Chena River on Easter Sunday, ca. 1905. PHOTO COURTESY OF CANDY WAUGAMAN.

17. CHILDREN'S CLOTHING

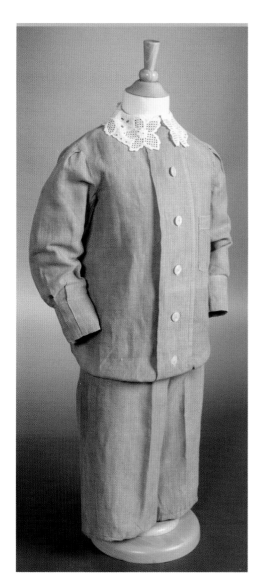

During the Victorian and early Edwardian eras, little boys wore smocks and dresses for several years before graduating to pants and suits. Children's clothing during those periods resembled miniaturized replicas of the current adult fashions.

Around 1910, parents began to dress their children like children, rather than small adults. Children's clothing became less restrictive and included rompers and more practical playwear. Pink and blue began to be associated with genders in the 1910s, the same time that manufactured clothing for children became readily available.

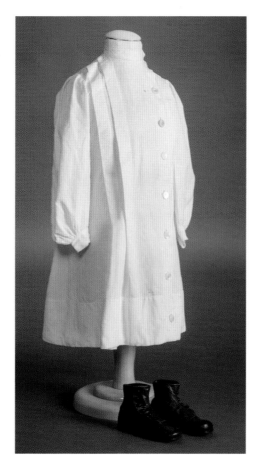

■ **RIGHT:** Many infant boys and girls wore white christening gowns for their baptisms. Typically made from fine white linen or cotton, christening gowns were usually hand-sewn by a mother during her pregnancy. Many, like this ca. 1890–1910 cotton christening gown from Barbara Cerny's collection, became family heirlooms.

■ **LEFT:** ca. 1895 boy's dress.

■ **ABOVE:** ca. 1910 boy's blue cotton suit with lace collar, cuffed sleeves, and matching knickerbockers. Lace collars on boy's outfits became wildly popular when the "Little Lord Fauntleroy" suit was introduced in the 1880s.

Girls' Dresses
Charming frocks for little lasses

During the Depression, hemlines for little girls' dresses reached above the knees. Bloomers were an important accessory for these short frocks. Although a defined waistline had returned to women's fashion by 1930, this was not the case for all girls' dresses.

Beginning in the mid-1930s, girls' fashion was greatly influenced by the child actress, Shirley Temple. Favorite frocks had puffed sleeves and were trimmed with simple decorative elements, including embroidery.

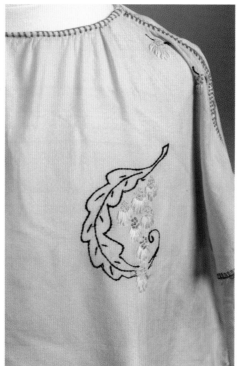

■ ABOVE: ca. 1929-1930 girl's toddler dress worn by Marjorie Logan Adams, Barbara Cerny's mother.
■ FAR LEFT: ca. 1930 girl's silk crepe dress with lace ruffle details and a ca. 1930 girl's smocked dress with embroidered trim and leaf designs.

■ LEFT: Detail from 1930 girl's smock. Embroidery, lace, ribbon, and multiple frills of organdy, lace, or ribbon were favorite decorations for girls' dresses in the 1930s.

■ ABOVE: Women and children dressed up for the Fourth of July festivities in Flat, Alaska in 1914. PHOTO COURTESY OF CANDY WAUGAMAN.

THE THOMAS CAR USED BY THE AMERICAN AUTOISTS
IN THE RACE ARROUND THE WORLD.
VALDEZ, ALASKA APR 9 09.

ACKNOWLEDGMENTS

First and foremost, I want to thank Barbara and Tim Cerny for letting me work with their remarkable fashion collection and supporting this book's publication. They made the photography shoots run smoothly, provided input throughout the writing and design process, and allowed me to work on the book from afar. Barb played an enormous role by collaborating on the costume research and descriptions, and by reviewing numerous drafts of the manuscript and layout.

Many thanks to Greg Martin for his wonderful photography and our fun interactions during the shoots. I also thank Michael Craft, Ronn Murray, and Brian Bohannon for their photographic contributions. Amy Hansen provided invaluable assistance during the photo sessions and graciously agreed to be our cover model. I am also grateful for the assistance of Willy Vinton, Brad Dietrich, Rod Benson, Michael Lecorchik, and Bob Miller during the photography sessions.

Candy Waugaman, Jan Plaquet, Jeff Mahl, and Joan Skilbred generously provided historic photographs for the book. I was fortunate to draw upon prior research and several costume descriptions by Abbie Cucolo and Kristin Summerlin. Derik Price helped with many aspects of the project, from locating photos in my old files to assisting with logistics for the photography sessions. Joe Faulhaber, Phyllis Movius and Connie Stricks were very helpful with their reviews of the manuscript.

I am forever indebted to Kent Sturgis for his guidance and publication management. Once again, Betty Watson worked her magic on the book's design, turning my crude mock-up into a work of art.

Finally, I extend heartfelt appreciation to my husband, Jim. I am richly blessed to have such a wise and caring partner who is not only supportive of my work, but is also skilled at restoring old photographs for my books. Thanks for the help, love.

Nancy DeWitt
Fairbanks, Alaska

■ **FACING PAGE: This Thomas Flyer was one of the first cars in Alaska, arriving in Valdez via steamship on April 9, 1908 during the famous New York-to-Paris Auto Race. It was the first automobile most people in Valdez had ever seen. The American team generously allowed the locals, including these ladies in their fancy hats, to sit in the car. It was shipped back to Seattle the following day, unable to leave the dock because of deep snow on the wagon trail. PHOTO COURTESY OF JEFF MAHL.**

WEDGEWOOD  RESORT

HOME OF THE FOUNTAINHEAD ANTIQUE AUTO MUSEUM

Wedgewood Resort is a destination in itself. This beautiful, 105-acre resort includes guest rooms at Bear Lodge, 305 residential-style suites, and a 75-acre wildlife sanctuary surrounding Wander Lake. All are conveniently situated just minutes from downtown Fairbanks.

Wedgewood Resort offers guests the opportunity to enjoy Alaskan art and photographic exhibits lining hallways and lobbies. We encourage guests to stroll along through beautifully landscaped grounds and relax on the observation decks overlooking Wander Lake. On winter nights, enjoy the surreal beauty of the northern lights.

Perhaps the most fascinating attraction at Wedgewood Resort is the antique auto and fashion museum. This remarkable attraction is just a short walk or courtesy van ride from any building on the resort's campus.

For further information about Wedgewood Resort, visit www.fountainheadhotels.com or call 800-528-4916.